This Book is

Protected by Instant IP

RAISING DREAMERS

WHY IMAGINATION IS THE KEY TO PRESERVING HUMANITY IN THE AGE OF ARTIFICIAL INTELLIGENCE

RAISING DREAMERS

WHY IMAGINATION IS THE KEY TO PRESERVING HUMANITY IN THE AGE OF ARTIFICIAL INTELLIGENCE

Wylde Scott

ethos
collective

Raising Dreamers © 2026 by Wylde Scott. All rights reserved.

Printed in the United States of America
Published by Igniting Souls
PO Box 43, Powell, OH 43065
IgnitingSouls.com

This book contains material protected under international and federal copyright laws and treaties. Any unauthorized reprint or use of this material is prohibited. No part of this book may be reproduced or transmitted in any form or by any means, electronic or mechanical, including photocopying, recording, or by any information storage and retrieval system, without express written permission from the author.

Library of Congress Control Number: 2025926868

Paperback ISBN: 978-1-63680-579-5
Hardcover ISBN: 978-1-63680-580-1
e-Book ISBN: 978-1-63680-584-9

Available in paperback, hardcover, e-book, and audiobook.

Any Internet addresses (websites, blogs, etc.) and telephone numbers printed in this book are offered as a resource. They are not intended in any way to be or imply an endorsement by Igniting Souls, nor does Igniting Souls vouch for the content of these sites and numbers for the life of this book.

Some names and identifying details may have been changed
to protect the privacy of individuals.

The content of this book reflects the author's personal experiences, opinions, and interpretations. The inclusion of any individual, living or deceased, or any organization or entity, is not intended to malign, defame, or harm the reputation of such persons or entities. All statements regarding individuals are solely the author's perspective and do not represent verified facts
unless expressly cited to a verifiable source.

The publisher has not independently investigated or confirmed the accuracy of any such references and disclaims all responsibility for them. Nothing in this book should be construed as factual assertions about the character, conduct, or reputation of any individual or entity mentioned. Any resemblance to persons living or dead is purely coincidental unless explicitly stated.

The publisher expressly disclaims liability for any alleged loss, damage, or injury arising from any perceived defamatory content or reliance upon statements within this work. Responsibility for the views, depictions, and representations rests solely with the author.

DEDICATION

For my first true believers, Maria Scheel,
Michael Jefferson, and Ryan "Flash" Bennett.

All failures of the future will be
failures of the imagination.

—*Wylde Scott*

TABLE OF CONTENTS

Introduction................................xi

Chapter 1   It's Their World........................ 1

Chapter 2   The Building Blocks of Imagination 27

Chapter 3   Brain Anatomy and Function 38

Chapter 4   The Real Process of Imagination 53

Chapter 5   The Captain of Our Own Ship 70

Chapter 6   Training the Little Conductor 105

Chapter 7   The Wylde Environment................ 150

A Few Words from the Author.................... 185

Wylde Scott.................................. 187

The Imagination Project......................... 191

References and Resources........................ 195

Endnotes 197

Acknowledgments 201

INTRODUCTION

In the 2008 animated film, *WALL-E* by Pixar Animation Studios, a small robot is left alone on Earth to clean up the mess left by humans, who have littered the planet with their waste and rendered it uninhabitable. All that remains of humanity has left Earth and lives on a giant cruise spaceship, awaiting a safe return to the planet. On board, humans have every convenience at their disposal. They do not have to worry about clothing, food, shelter, or employment. Technology has evolved to the point where the very act of reaching for a drink has become too difficult to bear.

Any of this sound familiar?

What has always been striking to me was how prophetic the filmmakers were in imagining what our future might look like. With all the abundance on Earth, what have humans done with it? With all the conveniences on the ship, what has become of humans? If you haven't seen the film, you should. It's a beautiful story that warms the heart and leaves us hope that we can save ourselves.

I won't walk you through the entire film, but I did want to point out some interesting parallels. The humans float around on space-age lounge chairs while advertising and messaging are blasted at them from all directions. They live with a screen no more than six inches in front of their face, which is split between ad space, entertainment, and communication with their friends. Large speakers flank their ears, and they are oblivious to the outside world as they chat away about nonsense. Every person on board is so obese and stationary that their bones have atrophied down to what a toddler might look like in the early stages of development.

While Wall-E is the central hero to the story, the ship captain plays a large part in the turn of events. In a fierce battle with the robot controlling the ship, he fights to help Wall-E trigger the ship's return to Earth. As the robot argues that humanity has far better odds of survival by remaining in space, the captain cries out, "I don't want to survive, I want to live!"

It makes me think of the choice we are all staring down at this very moment.

When I started to write this book, it was always about imagination. Imagination is responsible for all the most wonderful advancements in human history. It was never just intelligence or math or science that drove us forward, but a single spark that goes out into the universe and drags an entire generation into a new and exciting direction. Between 1900 and 1908, more than five hundred car companies were formed in the United States, but only Henry Ford conceived the assembly line. Before that fateful day in 1903 when the Wright brothers flew their first airplane on the beaches of Kitty Hawk, North Carolina, humans had spent centuries dreaming of flight. Individual inventors and researchers had been working on different versions of the airplane for nearly fifty years. There were nearly three hundred years between the time when English scientist William Gilbert coined the term "electricus" in 1600 and when Thomas Edison invented the lightbulb in 1879. What kept us in the dark for so long?

I have never understood, with the immense power and importance of imagination, why we spend so little time on imagination. Why is it a footnote in the curriculum of primary schools around the world? Why do we fill the heads of toddlers with tales of Easter bunnies and Santa Claus, simply to tear it all down the minute they turn six? Why is it not at the top of every list in every house and every school district in every country on earth? My original intent was to advocate for bringing imagination back into childhood and create a central role in the daily development of the next generation. But something happened on the way to the forum: Artificial Intelligence (AI).

We are standing at the threshold of an era unlike any other before us. Artificial Intelligence has reached supersonic speed, bringing with it the promise of an entirely new level of civilization. In July 2025, with the release of Grok-4, X-AI's Large Language model, Elon Musk announced that testing showed a level of intelligence smarter than PhDs in every field simultaneously. The Grok-4 model was achieving perfect scores on the SATs, the GREs, and nearly every mathematical test known to man. Large language models are beating world champions in chess and Go. In an interview, Eric Schmidt, the former CEO of Google, stated that virtually everyone will have the equivalent of Leonardo Da Vinci and Albert Einstein in their pocket.

The speed of this transformation will increase. What many may not realize is that we are witnessing the Manhattan Project of our times unfold right before our eyes. All of the brightest minds in every country are being abducted into an arms race. Previously unheard-of technologists are being offered superstar contracts in the hundreds of millions, usually reserved for the greatest sports stars and movie legends. Wall Street and Silicon Valley are laying down bets of billions of dollars, in some cases, before a single line of code is even written. AI itself is so smart that it is being enlisted to multiply the efficiencies and trajectory at which we scale. With that kind of firepower, it's a virtual guarantee that we will achieve many of the innovations only dreamed about by our forefathers. Flying cars, robotaxis, personal AI assistants, and robots are all coming online as we speak.

But what about humanity? Like Newton's Third Law of Motion, for every action, there is an equal and opposite reaction. With every advancement we make, we will face challenges that no previous generation has faced. If technology can do all of the jobs that once required college graduates, and robots reach a level of physical dexterity that can replace plumbers and mechanics, what happens to our jobs? We can't all be coders. AI is already better than 99 percent of the coders on the planet. Price Waterhouse says over 30 percent of jobs will be replaced by AI. Goldman Sachs predicts that three hundred million will be replaced or downgraded. According to McKinsey, by 2030, at least 14 percent of employees across the globe might need to change their careers. If no one has a job, how do we pay our bills? And if no one has a job, what will people do? Everyone is asking these questions. Unfortunately, to this point, there aren't a whole lot of satisfactory answers.

If you think this might be some sort of doomsday rant predicting the fall of humanity, you should know that I am an eternal optimist. I share what Peter Diamandis, the founder of the XPrize and one of our most revered futurists, calls an abundance mindset. I believe in all possibilities. My argument isn't that we turn off computers, roll back innovation, and return to another dark age. I have always believed that the answer lies in our imagination. The answer lies in our ability to innovate our way through any challenge we create. Like we have seen so many times before in history—the enlightenment, the industrial revolution, the digital revolution—we are capable of rising to the

> I AM AN ETERNAL OPTIMIST…
> I BELIEVE IN ALL POSSIBILITIES.

occasion as a species. But if we hope to do more than survive this next transition, we must move forward with intention.

Before we dive into the premise of this book, think about the last twenty years as evidence of the urgency we face. The last great turn of the digital revolution began at the dawn of this century with the introduction of the iPhone. With the amazing vision of Steve Jobs came an entirely new way of communicating and experiencing life. The iPhone has transformed human interaction throughout the world. You can sit at a café and chat with people you barely know in any one of fifty countries. You can watch hours of entertainment or listen to your favorite music on demand. You can order food from hundreds of restaurants in your city, or have products delivered to your house from companies across the globe. You can have cars pick you up and take you where you please. All with a tap on the screen. But what have we lost in trade for all this incredible convenience?

In the last twenty years, we have seen our literacy and numeracy rates plummet across all levels of education. While social media promised a more connected world, an entire generation reports being lonelier than ever. Rates of anxiety, depression, addiction, and suicide have skyrocketed. Our answer to everything? Medicate everyone. What we are witnessing is the complete breakdown of the human connection. Why was the movie *WALL-E* so prophetic? Because, fifteen years later, we are witnessing many of the outcomes the movie predicted. As innovators, we may have delivered, but as a society, we missed the mark. In many ways, we failed to protect our most valuable resource—our children.

Tristan Harris, co-founder of the Center for Humane Technology and a prominent technology ethicist, summarizes our current predicament as follows:

> So just to summarize, we're currently releasing the most powerful, inscrutable, uncontrollable technology that humanity has ever invented, that's already demonstrating the behaviors of self-preservation and deception that we thought only existed in sci-fi movies. We're releasing it faster than we've released any other technology in history, and under the maximum incentive to cut corners on safety, and we're doing this because we think it will lead to utopia. Now there's a word for what we're doing right now, which is this is: insane.[1]

We are facing a great paradox: As the world becomes more abundant and we have less need to entertain new thoughts and ideas simply for the sake of survival, the actual number of people inclined toward innovation will become smaller. At the same time, the complexity of our challenges as a species continues to increase. A continually changing world forever drives the need for continued innovation. Even if we are successful in resolving the economic and logistical challenges of an AI-led society, we are still facing a crisis of purpose and happiness, which at its core is the center of what we consider to be human.

The news isn't all bad.

We might just be living through the greatest period of creativity in human history. Just like Athens in the fourth century BC, Florence during the Medici era, or the Paris art scene in the 1800s, we will see a flourishing of human capability. But all of this wonderful promise could hold one more advantage: The opportunity to return childhood to our children and restore the human connection. All we have to do is use our imagination.

I'm a children's author. I spend my days and nights thinking about their future. The purpose of this book is to address the complexity of the world they are approaching and offer solutions on how we can build young minds that are capable of not only surviving but thriving in the twenty-first century.

While the methods discussed in the following chapters are heavily geared toward children, the knowledge and techniques can help anyone rebuild their imagination, enhance their creativity, develop the skills needed to succeed in the future, find purpose, and improve mental health and happiness.

I hope to accomplish seven things:

1. Convince parents, teachers, and everyone else that imagination is the most valuable skill set in the twenty-first century and the key to maintaining humanity.
2. Raise the profile of Imagination and Play to the top of everyone's list.
3. Reframe imagination and creativity away from the idea that these are simply inherent talents gifted only to a few—into trainable, usable toolsets that everyone can deploy.
4. Help everyone understand how imagination, creativity, and innovation work (what I'll refer to as the mechanics) and how to develop them at any age.
5. Connect the dots from imagination and creativity to the foundations of purpose and happiness.
6. Convince everyone of the critical stages between the ages of five and ten as a unique one-time opportunity to permanently hardwire in a mental framework that will last a lifetime.
7. Provide readers with a roadmap and a fundamental tool kit with techniques to move from research and theory into actionable items and activities.

> I am excited you have picked up this book.
> Come, take this journey with me.
>
> —Wylde Scott

Chapter 1

IT'S THEIR WORLD

SOME GOOD ADVICE...

Not so long ago, I had a friend who was a data and automation specialist for one of the largest technology companies in the world. Around the time of our friendship, he invented a significant piece of technology that changed his career trajectory entirely. He went from being a mild-mannered worker bee amongst the crowd to rockstar status within the company. His daily routine changed from long hours chained to the desk to dog-and-pony shows around the world. Salespeople dragged him into presentations with global giants and world governments to explain his technology and how it could help them solve some of their biggest challenges. Occasionally, he'd come home, and we'd have hours-long chats. Along with tales of amazing countries, fancy restaurants, and world-class hotels, he'd share some insider knowledge about these life-changing projects. I was fascinated, but at times frightened. Tucked in between these tales, he would constantly make pronouncements like "this industry is dead," "forget about that, it won't exist anymore," and "wait till you see what's coming." Being an advocate for children, I would try to frame his stories around what their world would look like. Lamenting the loss of so many things I held dear in my own mind, I would constantly share with him:

"I worry about their future."

His response would always be the same:

"You have to stop thinking about their world being like your own. Their world will be different. If you want them to survive, they must be able to live in the world that's coming."

For those born in the twentieth century, it will be difficult to let go of what was. It took me a while, but I've finally come around to understanding the reality of his words. Today is the last day you will ever live in the past. The future doesn't start tomorrow; it's already here, staring you in the face. If we want our children to succeed in the twenty-first century, they have to be able to operate in the twenty-first century, with all its blessings, dangers, and pitfalls. The key to understanding much of this book is to let go of the past and embrace a mindset built for the future. Like my forward-thinking friend, you are going to hear me pronounce a lot of the twentieth century as "dead" or irrelevant. If you are not already there, I hope you will be by the end of this book. Your children are depending on it.

So what does the remainder of the twenty-first century look like?

If you're an optimist, many of the science-fiction fantasies of flying cars, sky cities, robot maids, and automatic food preparation live in your head. It's like a wonderful version of the 1960s cartoon *The Jetsons*. If you're a pessimist, your vision is likely to look like something out of the 1984 sci-fi movie *Terminator*. Skynet, the film's version of Artificial Intelligence, controls everything and perceives humans as a risk. Robots are sent to terminate the human race.

But what's the reality? Likely a little of both. One of the great hallmarks of the twenty-first century will be its incredible unpredictability.

The eight-hundred-pound gorilla currently driving all our conversations is Artificial Intelligence (AI) and its impact on the world. Over the last three years, we have all been fascinated with the introduction of Large Language Models, the most famous being OpenAI's ChatGPT. Early versions of LLMs were trained to compress all of the world's knowledge into a database accessible to anyone who had a computer or cell phone. ChatGPT gained more than one hundred million active users within two months of its release in November 2022. Currently, the platform has over four hundred million active users, with 122 million users processing more than one billion queries per day. Its primary function for most of the general public has been either Google on steroids, with people asking it to search for things they want to know, or, in many cases, as a college paper writer for people wanting to offload basic thinking and writing tasks. But all of that is rapidly changing...

ChatGPT itself has been working feverishly behind the scenes, improving the speed and accuracy of its models and launching a world of innovative functionality. Meanwhile, a multitude of competitors and new companies have emerged over the last twelve months, offering new products to the market. Within an eighteen-month period, Elon Musk's Xai was able to move from launch to Grok 4, surpassing all previous models with its capabilities.

While industry experts and armchair quarterbacks alike argue over whether these models actually have the ability to reason, AI has moved from "thinking" into "doing." The industry has quickly progressed from learning, analyzing, and regurgitating data to performing tasks. Not only can it write your papers, but it can also perform many duties once requiring higher education or advanced degrees. With the introduction of Agentic AI, commonly referred to as "Agents" or "personal AI assistants," current models can do your taxes, write legal documents, design your marketing strategies and materials, play chess, organize your photos, make dinner reservations, and code your next website. As I write this chapter, OpenAI just entered their reasoning model in the AtCoder World Finals, which brought together the twelve best coders in the world. In 2024, AI models ranked ten thousandth globally in coding competitions. In 2025, second place to what might be the last human coder standing.

2025 will be the year that AI changed *everything*...

If AI is the eight-hundred-pound gorilla, then the elephant in the room is job loss. Companies all over the world are rushing at light speed to understand and implement any AI strategy that might add to their capabilities, improve their market position, or increase their speed and efficiency. The long list of college-educated, white-collar jobs currently queueing up on the chopping block has taken everyone by surprise:

- Accountants and Bookkeepers
- Lawyers and Legal Aides
- Executive Assistants
- Scientists and Research Assistants
- Low-level Engineers and Architects
- Marketing Professionals
- Video Producers
- Editors
- Diagnostic Technicians
- Middle Managers

While at the highest level, technology leaders are in heavy thought about impacts of AI's march into higher and higher levels of intelligence such as Artificial General Intelligence (AGI), where machines move from merely mimicking human intelligence into being as smart as humans, to Artificial Super Intelligence (ASI), where machines are more intelligent than all humans combined, more practical conversations are focused around AI's next move. At the functional level, predictability is the next high ground. The tactical goal is for machines to move from mimicking our thoughts and completing tasks based on requests to predicting what we want and taking initiative on their own to complete tasks without our involvement. This is playing out in several ways, but I think a far more critical aspect of the AI revolution is the move of AI into the physical realm.

THE RISE OF THE ROBOTS...

On a recent episode of *American Optimist*, a podcast hosted by Joe Lonsdale, a prominent Silicon Valley figure and co-founder of Palantir, I ran across a foretelling example. Joe was chatting with Boris Sofman, a serial technologist and entrepreneur, who is transforming the entire construction industry. Through his company Bedrock Robotics, Sofman is taking much of the knowledge and experience he gained through years invested at Waymo, Google's self-driving car company, and converting construction equipment, such as cranes, excavators, loaders, and dump trucks, into autonomous, self-operating machines. If Bedrock succeeds in its mission, which is the most likely outcome, entire construction and earth-moving projects will be able to run efficiently with little or no human intervention. In the most remote regions of the planet, these projects can be run through satellite technology. The benefits include savings in the trillions of dollars across the globe, better efficiency, and increased safety, but what happens to the truck driver, the crane operator, and the site manager?

> **AI WILL EVENTUALLY MANAGE AND MONITOR ITSELF.**

This scenario will play out time and time again. Today, we already have factories largely run by robotic arms and automated assembly lines requiring only a fraction of the number of workers as in previous generations. Bank branches are becoming a thing of the past as 99 percent of financial transactions occur in the cloud. When was the last time you stepped into a bank because you needed to deposit a paycheck, pay a bill, or apply for a loan? Some people will still find their value in the technology loop. Perhaps factory plant managers who understand how to monitor and manage AI systems, or mechanics who repair robots. But with AI as intelligent as humans moving into the physical space, it's almost a long-term guarantee that AI will eventually manage and monitor itself.

Imagine a new fleet of robotaxis in any large city. The taxi itself knows when it needs an oil change or repair and schedules its own maintenance. It then drives itself back to the shop, where robots, physically capable and sufficiently trained, remove the necessary parts and replace them with new ones. The taxi's diagnostic system runs its own check and approves the vehicle to return to the street. The robotaxi is back to picking up passengers without a single human involved. Meanwhile, a computer looks at the entire fleet as a whole, knows how many taxis are on the road, and where they are. It understands traffic patterns and time spans. It knows the personal schedules of its passengers and who needs to be where and when.

With the innovations at companies like Bedrock, there is no reason to believe that AI in combination with robotics won't begin to replace the majority of jobs in the physical space:

Plumbers
Mechanics
Electricians
Drivers

SAY HELLO TO GARY...

During Tesla's Q2 2025 earnings call, Elon Musk stated that the company plans to scale production of its Optimus Robot as quickly as possible, aiming for a million units per year within the next five years. He believes the price will eventually drop to an affordable range of $20,000–$30,000 each and hinted at a goal of one hundred thousand Optimus robots produced per month by 2030. Musk believes Optimus will find applications in various settings, including factories and homes, and can perform complex tasks such as twenty-four-hour care for quadriplegics. Musk sees the financing of these robots much like a car or cell phone, where no one actually buys the machine; they simply pay the lowest possible monthly fee for it. At least ten other companies are competing globally to introduce humanoid robots into the market. What is striking about the latest models is not just their physical qualities; every one will be loaded with the most advanced AI known to humankind.

Children born in 2025 are likely to watch this play out to its full potential before they reach adulthood. Imagine if you will, what it would be like to have a personal robot at your disposal. For the sake of this example, we'll call our robot *Gary*. Gary will be wirelessly connected to the cloud and have the ability to seamlessly operate between the physical and non-physical space. With advancements in natural language, all you would have to do is speak, and any one of a thousand tasks is complete without any effort on your part.

> *Gary, I'm hungry. Can you please order a pizza?*

> *Gary, can you tell me what it costs to fly to New York this Saturday?*

> *Gary, can you see what's going on with the drain in the shower?*

> *Gary, can you read War and Peace to me?*

> *Gary, can you massage my feet?*

Gary, I want a new house. Can you please look at everything available within thirty miles within my price range, show me the top ten you think I will like, ask the bank how much they'll lend me and what the payments will be, contact the agent, and make an offer based on the most square feet for the lowest payment with the best view, let me know when the offer is accepted, arrange for the movers and let me know when we will be in the new house? Thank You.

Poor Gary. You won't even have to ask Gary to perform daily tasks like cleaning and cooking. The house will always be perfectly clean due to automated programming. Gary never sleeps and never gets tired. Gary can work twenty-four hours, seven days a week, can recharge himself, and self-repair any worn-out parts. Gary can handle running whatever business you have for you. He can even serve as your bodyguard.

If everyone or every house has a Gary and every company uses physical or machine-based robots to complete all of these tasks, what jobs will even exist in twenty or thirty years? Here's another way of looking at it: your job won't exist because it's just not needed anymore. Have you seen ads posted lately looking for horse and buggy drivers? What about lamplighters, milkmen, town criers, or typewriter repairmen? Do you even know what a Slubber Doffer is?

If that's not unsettling enough for you, I'll share one more wrinkle:

THE SPEED OF CHANGE

An old professor I knew at the end of the last century was obsessed with this idea. He would say, "The thing is, what will affect all of these students, more than anything else in their lifetime, will be the speed of change." He was so right about so many things. I miss him dearly.

If you are a child in the twenty-first century, much of your life could be like having a rug pulled out from under you every time you walk into a room. Not only do we not know what jobs will be available in twenty years, we're not even sure what is going to happen in the next three.

If you are watching the incredible trajectory of Artificial Intelligence, you know what I am talking about. Every two weeks, a new victor is announced in the race for supremacy. One week it's ChatGPT 4.0, the next week it's DeepSeek, and then the next it's Grok4. Can't wait to see what happens with release numbers 6, 7, 8, 9, and 10! If you are over thirty and trying to learn how to use many of these technologies, the world is confusing. What exactly is Perplexity? What does it do? Is that the same thing as Claude? Can't I just use Instagram? Just tell me what those guys used for that Bigfoot video.

I recently saw a video clip with Sam Altman, the founder of OpenAI. The interviewer asked what advice he would give someone who is around twenty-five years old today. His response went something like this:

> It's funny how quickly the world went from telling twenty or twenty-five-year-olds to "learn to program." So, programming doesn't matter. Learn AI tools. I wonder what will be next because, of course, something will be next…"

Altman's words trailed out with his thoughts. "I believe that skills like resilience, adaptability, creativity are the skills that will pay off in the next couple of decades."

The smartest guys in the room can't tell us exactly what *careers* we should be preparing for. On a different podcast, Peter Diamandis recently interviewed Eric Schmidt. Their conversation drifted into AI's capabilities around fast learning loops. The latest and greatest trend for companies looking to succeed in this lightning round of survival is AI-based, self-learning, action-oriented feedback loops embedded in every aspect of your company. The process goes something like this. You monitor every part of your business in *real time*, make adjustments on the fly, analyze the results of those adjustments, make even further changes based on the results, then repeat the process endlessly and forever. One piece of technology can do what would have otherwise required hundreds, if not thousands, of employees. Companies will rise and fall in the blink of an eye based on who identifies and implements change the fastest. The leaderboard will constantly change. No company is safe. One thing they all agree on? Human beings do not have the capability to compete at this speed.

So what on earth do all of us humans do in a world of hyper-automation and robotic assistants? What do we train for if no one knows what jobs will exist, and everything we train for could be made obsolete overnight anyway?

THE TWENTY-FIRST-CENTURY MIND

Ok. I am going to make my first pronouncement of a twentieth-century concept that is dead and gone and needs to be buried in the graveyard: The Job.

If you want your child to have a fighting chance in the twenty-first century, you need to reframe all of your thinking around the twenty-first-century mindset, which requires three types of intelligence.

As illustrated in Figure 1 below, the mental framework for a child in the coming century will be at the confluence of Organic, Artificial, and Creative Intelligence.

Figure 1

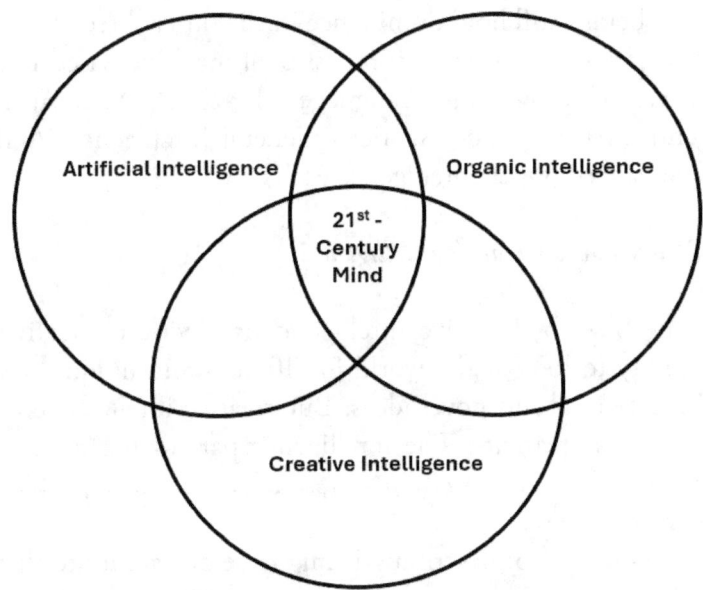

Organic Intelligence is the natural intelligence we are all born with or develop throughout our lifetime. It includes:

IQ: Our traditional measure of cognitive ability. Problem-Solving and Academic Performance.

EQ (Emotional Quotient): Our emotional awareness. Our ability to communicate and empathize.

SQ (Social Quotient): Our ability to manage relationships, work with others, and assume leadership.

AQ (Adversity Quotient): Our ability to withstand and adapt to change.

IQ is the main form of human intelligence in competition with and being replaced by Artificial intelligence. For now, human beings still hold dominance in the other three.

Artificial intelligence encompasses all machine-based intelligence, including Large Language Models (LLMs), Agents (Agentic AI), Robotics, Artificial General Intelligence (AGI), and Advanced Super Intelligence (ASI).

But what is *Creative Intelligence*?

The base for Creative Intelligence is obviously creativity, the ability to look at the world in different and unique ways, and create new and novel ideas. But creative intelligence isn't the same as creativity. The intelligence part of the term is a measure of our ability to *apply* those talents to solve problems and create value.

The old way of describing it might be our ability to think "outside the box." The newer, more fashionable term people are using these days is *high agency*. All of these terms revolve in some form or another around the concept that it's not what we *know*, but what *we can do with what we know*.

With Artificial Intelligence surpassing our own abilities of knowledge and problem-solving, and systems already being trained to mimic the more human aspects of intelligence, such as emotional responses, empathy, and communication, Creative Intelligence becomes the last stronghold of human value on earth. Our ability to imagine and innovate is the key to our very survival.

INTELLIGENCE VS. VALUE

Another aspect of twentieth-century thinking that must change is the foundation of being *smart*. There will always be people smarter than you. There's always some genius around the corner who can solve an equation or figure out the square root of something quicker than you can. But guess what? If we measure how smart we are by what exams we can pass, AI will outsmart us all.

Our entire cultural and economic systems are based on a ladder of education predicated on the belief that what matters most is how we perform on tests. In chapter 6, we will spend time examining why that is and why that model no longer holds any value in the twenty-first century. The biggest question we should be asking is whether our children will be *effective* in their world. It amazes me that, with all the incredible evidence to the contrary, we continue to cling to the twentieth-century hierarchies. None of the industrialists who built this country were college-educated. Many of the minds currently leading technological innovations dropped out of or never went to college. We must shift our bias away from ivory tower academics and toward real-world applications.

I have a friend who is one of the most fascinating characters on Earth. He was raised in the American South and is prone to expressing himself in southern colloquialisms and pithy "sayins". To give a little more relevance, this friend has little time for anything that doesn't have practical use or significance. Rules don't matter, intelligence doesn't matter, and your opinion doesn't matter if it can't get the job done. One of my favorite aphorisms that comes out of his mouth goes something like this: "Mama always said, how smart you are depends on what part of the world you're standing in." In layman's terms, what good does your law degree do when you are standing in the desert with a busted radiator and two flat tires?

The idea of spending the first eighteen to twenty-five years of your life simply preparing for a job by following a straight line makes no sense moving forward.

The single most important measurement in the twenty-first century will be whether or not you add *value*. Value is the only measurement that will matter. It doesn't really matter whether you open a tiny bakery on the corner or you are trying to solve quantum physics. If a machine or another person can do it better, faster, or cheaper, you are likely going to struggle to find economic relevance. On the flip side, if people line up around the corner to buy the best-tasting chocolate-nutmeg-almond croissant from you, AI will have a much harder time replacing you.

So what skills will be needed in the twenty-first century, and how do we train for them?

TWENTY-FIRST-CENTURY SKILLS

Let me start by introducing what I call the AA battery. The future belongs to the people who are both *autotelic* and *autodidactic*. This will be the jetpack of the twenty-first century.

Autotelic is a fancy way of saying people who do things because they want to. They do things because they find them enjoyable. They do things often for the sake of doing them, and they can be lost for hours in the effort.

Another way of saying this is that rather than being driven by external motivations, such as the expectations of parents or teachers, children need to be driven by *intrinsic motivation,* where the desire to do something comes from inside.

Picasso didn't need anyone to tell him to paint. Shakespeare didn't need anyone to tell him to write. No one told Jeff Bezos he had to start Amazon, or Elon Musk that he needed to start a rocket company. No one told Steve Jobs he needed to start Apple.

There are entire books written on the subject, but later in this book, we will attempt to make connections for you on what really drives intrinsic motivation.

Autodidactic is a term for people who can learn on their own, without formal guidance or instruction. In my opinion, this has been one of the most successful attributes of modern technology. With the internet, information on almost every subject became widely available to nearly everyone. The cost of acquiring knowledge has literally gone to zero. What AI has done is to accelerate the speed and increase the breadth and depth of available knowledge.

The high-end version of this might be learning advanced chemistry through a program like the Khan Academy. My favorite examples are far simpler. Let's take cooking as an example. If you want to make the best lasagna you have ever tasted, you can ask ChatGPT or Google or any other search algorithm for both the ingredients and the recipe. But if you really want to learn how to make it, the best way is usually to watch a step-by-step video. I'm guessing many of you have already done this. You hit up your phone for the ingredients while at the store, then prop up the phone next to your stove while you cook.

The idea of High Agency is embedded in the AA battery. Rather than wait for some form of external mandate or pressure telling you what to do, or wade through years of very expensive schooling completely irrelevant to the things you care about and wish to pursue, you simply learn what you need to learn based on what you find interesting.

The AA Battery is a great framework for describing the personality most likely to succeed in the twenty-first century, but it's not a complete list of skills that will be needed to thrive.

TOP TWENTY-FIRST-CENTURY SKILLS

Everyone is producing lists. The World Economic Forum just produced its list of the highest-in-demand skills for 2025. They also introduced the following list of skills on the rise by 2030.

1. Creative thinking
2. Analytical thinking
3. Technology literacy
4. Curiosity and lifelong learning
5. Resilience, flexibility, and adaptability
6. Systems thinking
7. AI and Big Data
8. Motivation and self-awareness
9. Talent Management
10. Service orientation and customer service

This list has been radically realigned over the last several years. You'll notice specific skills, like mathematics, history, or any of the things commonly taught through traditional education, are missing. Also striking is the ascendance of far more esoteric skill sets, such as creative thinking, curiosity, lifelong learning, resilience, flexibility, and adaptability. I don't remember any of those classes in college. While the lists give us a guide as to what people believe will be needed, the challenge with the WEF list for example, is that it is still based on *jobs*. This list was gathered from CEOs and executives across fourteen hundred global companies. These same CEOs are the ones racing to implement AI and eliminate jobs.

Here are my top skills for the future:

1. Imagination and Creativity
2. Adaptability, Flexibility, and Resilience
3. Curiosity and Intrinsic Motivation
4. Critical Thinking and Problem Solving
5. Collaboration and Communication

I've intentionally limited this list to ten skills, organized in five related categories, to establish a hierarchy of value. To me, these are the most important skills we need to instill in our children during the early years of development. Everything else is secondary. AI fluency will be an important set of knowledge through the current transformation, but really, twenty years from now, you can just ask Gary what the best tool sets are, or he'll simply figure it out on his own.

As part of these top five skills, children will need to develop a set of supporting traits designed to help them master these skills.

1. Positive self-esteem.
2. An empowered psychology based on possibilities.
3. A love of exploration and learning.
4. A bias toward action.

5. An orientation toward goals and objectives.
6. Comfort with ambiguity and risk-taking.
7. The desire to seek alternatives.
8. Comfort with failure.

The book's remaining chapters will be dedicated to helping parents, educators, and society develop these skill sets and traits in the very young, with the belief that doing so will carry them through the challenges they will face as adults.

But before we move on, we need to introduce two more concepts: purpose and human connection.

PURPOSE

Everything is *connected*.

Two major disconnects will happen as a result of the AI transformation. One, what will people do *for a living*, and two, what will people *do*? These challenges are not one and the same.

We are coming out of a world where a person's identity is connected to the job they do. For example, I am a *Lawyer*, and I am a *Doctor*, I am a *Programmer*. Or in another form, ask people what they do, and they inevitably reference their Place of Employment. I work at Costco. I work at Google, or I work at American Airlines.

One of the greatest avenues for achieving mental health is when what you do is also who you are. Few among us have had the privilege of living with that sort of alignment. For most people on the planet, what they do all day is work. And work is a basic form of trade, *labor* in exchange for *money*. As we've already discussed, the disconnect between the loss of jobs and what people do for money is likely to create great disruption. In the transition, it will not be an easy challenge to resolve.

When pressed on this subject, the leaders of the AI movement generally go silent and offer up some basic response related to Universal Basic Income, or UBI. I cringe every time I hear these words. "Beware the man offering utopia" comes to my mind. No one has to work, and everyone has whatever they need. When pressed on how the economics of this system actually work, no one has an answer. Everyone agrees we need it. No one will agree on who's paying for it. The statement also belies the foundation of our current economic models. If there are no jobs, no one has money to buy things. If no one has money to buy things, companies can't afford to make things. It's an endless cycle of doom.

If everyone is supposed to get a robot, but no one can pay for the robot, how does the company pay for the factory and materials that make the robot? Should we look to the government? Well, if no one has a job, there is no income base for taxes. If no one is paying companies for their goods, you can't tax the producers. If we can't tax the consumers, and we can't tax the producers, where is all this wonderful money coming from for Universal Basic Income? We could just print money. Yeah, that'll work. Everyone is finally reaching the conclusion that we simply don't have the answer, and we need to come up with something entirely new. This sounds like the most important X Prize in history. But this book is not about economics.

Suppose we actually figure out how to make this utopia viable, and after a difficult transition period, we finally create an economic structure based on value. In a world of true abundance, where no one *has* to work, and everyone has whatever they need, a different crisis arises—a crisis of purpose.

In researching and developing this book, it was amazing how many correlations I found between the process of creating *value* and creating *purpose*.

> *Each of these is humanity being true to itself, a hummingbird is true to itself by building a nest, a peach tree by bearing fruit, and a nimbus cloud by producing rain.*
>
> —Rick Rubin, author of *The Creative Act*

Human beings aren't designed to sit around and do nothing. The twenty-first-century mindset and skills prescribed in this book have an unbelievable power to address the question of what people do. The foundation of constructing a vivid Imagination is, in many ways, the same foundation of mental health. The foundation involved in creativity is, likewise, the foundation of finding purpose.

Under the twentieth-century model, well-meaning parents and society as a whole unintentionally designed an overarching false dichotomy. The world for young people was set up as a false choice between "getting a good job" and "following your passion." Well, guess what? Without jobs, this isn't really going to be a problem anymore. Your parents never wanted you to be unhappy. They were just afraid you wouldn't be able to take care of yourself. And in the twentieth-century model, fields such as math and science, or careers like accounting and nursing, were far better guarantees of income. That model will not produce the same results in the twenty-first century. So, here's the silver lining: Everyone will be free to "follow their passion."

In a value-based economy, producing new products, services, or content where no one else can is the most viable path toward income. If income isn't the goal, then passion is the most likely road to lead you to purpose. If a job is no longer the goal, then purpose becomes king.

One of my favorite books around this subject is *Flow* by Mihaly Csikszentmihalyi, the Distinguished Professor of Psychology and Management at Claremont Graduate University.

Earlier, he served as the head of the department of psychology at the University of Chicago. He dedicated many years to studying happiness and creativity, and he based *Flow* on a theory he developed through years of research. Csikszentmihalyi believed that a person learns to enjoy life and find meaning through an ongoing stream of experiences. In his eyes, flow is the state of optimal experience, a state in which people are so involved in an activity that nothing else seems to matter. In his own words:

> "It is what a sailor holding a tight course feels when the wind rips through her hair, when the boat lunges through the waves like a colt, sails, hull, wind and sea humming in harmony that vibrates the sailor's veins."[2]

In basic terms, happiness is found most often through purpose, and purpose is found through the engagement of experiences we find both challenging and exhilarating. Purpose is an active pursuit, not a passive response. He foresaw the challenges we are now facing:

> "The complexity and freedom that have been thrust upon us, and that our ancestors have fought so hard to achieve, are a challenge we must find ways to master… There is no one who tells us, "Here is the goal worth spending your life on."[3]

I reference *Flow* because finding this type of purpose requires many of the skills and traits defined in this book: action, exploration, the ability to try new things and overcome fear, resilience, intrinsic motivation, and self-determination. These are similar skills and traits that will drive a value-based economy. In the process of intentionally building imaginative and creative young minds, we can also build in the same skill sets that will allow them to add value and find meaning.

In his book, *Creating Innovators,* Tony Wagner describes a path to purpose that I really believe in: Play → Passion → Purpose. He sees the path as a progression. Play and exploration lead to the discovery of passion; pursuing passions over time develops into purpose. In this book, we will explore how to implement this progression and other exercises that drive purpose in our daily lives.

HUMAN CONNECTION

> *Two roads diverged in a wood, and I—*
> *I took the one less traveled by,*
> *And that has made all the difference.*
>
> —Robert Frost, *The Road Not Taken*

No less important in the twenty-first century for our children will be protecting the human connection. We have already witnessed the results of the social media era, which resulted in isolation, anxiety, depression, and suicide. AI, and its long-term promise of no longer having to think, do, or act on anything, of never having to leave your house or see another human being, should you choose, has far greater potential to destroy human connections than anything in our previous existence. It will be highly tempting to let the machines do everything for us. And if the past is any indicator, we will far more easily trade AI's modern conveniences and benefits for our own self-agency. The results could be disastrous for humanity.

I want you to imagine two very different roads for a child born and raised in the twenty-first century:

On one path, we have the virtual reality, Meta- or Google-type universe. Like the spaceship-stranded Humans in *WALL-E*, our children live a life disconnected from what's around them. The AI universe has met all of their basic needs. They have no reason to leave the house. Their heads are filled with days of mindless content, video games, and propaganda. They are obese, lonely, and depressed. But don't worry, drugs to sedate and control them are readily available. These children offer no resistance. Within a generation, they will barely be able to think beyond the *Matrix*. The entire race has a high chance of extinction due to its own lack of procreation. No need for Skynet to end us, we'll do it ourselves.

Think I'm being dramatic?

I have a young friend named Spencer Podolski. Spencer is one of those rare birds that straddle the transition from Millennial to Generation Z. Like most of his generation, he was raised with technology. iPhones and social media are a regular part of his world and how it operates. But Spencer is different. He craves human connection and has decided to dedicate his entire soul to building deeper and lasting connections with people in the real world. He recently set up a new Instagram page handle called *thesocialswitch*. The goal is to bring the practice of being social back to social media. On his first post, Spencer offered up a meet-and-greet to a set of strangers at a dog park in Wilmington, North Carolina, his hometown. The post went viral and got several hundred thousand views in the first twenty-four hours. A couple of days later, about twenty strangers met for the first time. But the post wasn't finished. By the end of the week, the numbers had moved to nearly one million views with thousands of comments, likes, and shares. He decided to host a beach walk that weekend, and nearly fifty strangers showed up. Investors and social media companies are now contacting him to see how they might expand what he is doing to people in different cities. Spencer's message to me: "People are *dying* to connect."

So what's the other path? I call it the path of full engagement. The children are mentally healthy and extremely creative. They thrive on challenges and live for human connection. Their life is full of dynamic, interactive experiences with the world around them. Through creative intelligence, they can determine and share their own value with the world, and it compensates them accordingly. Artificial Intelligence is a toolset they use at their own discretion and will. It doesn't define them or own them. They can see and adjust to changes rapidly, and always maintain a positive mental state regardless of outcome. In essence, they are in control of the experience we call life, and are active participants in it.

Which path do you think future generations will follow? What if it's your child?

This is not a theory. This is preparation.

So why, with all of the serious concerns listed above, is Imagination the most important skill set of the twenty-first century?

IMAGINATION IS *EVERYTHING...*

Without imagination, there is no creativity.
Without imagination, there is no passion or meaningful purpose.
Without imagination, there is no independence of thought,
Without imagination, there are no possibilities,
Without possibilities, there is no hope.
Without hope, there is no humanity.

In the next few chapters, I am going to show you how to build, protect, and preserve the greatest gift ever given to humankind.

Chapter 2

THE BUILDING BLOCKS OF IMAGINATION

WHAT IS IMAGINATION?

In my research on imagination, I've noticed that many books begin with the question, What is imagination? I'm not going to spend much time on that. We all have an imagination. We're all born with it. We've all experienced an "Ah-ha!" moment, where something new pops into our heads and we're excited about its potential. So why do so many of us think we are not "creative"? What happens to the imagination we are born with as we grow older? I'll spend some time on that as we move through the chapters and take a deep dive into chapters 5 and 6.

Over the next three chapters, I'm going to focus on how it works, so that as we move into creating vivid imaginations, you have a solid framework for understanding the mechanics behind the actions we are taking with our children.

For the most basic framework on the concept of creative thinking, I'm really in love with the simple definition given by Sir Ken Robinson in his international bestseller *Creative Schools*.

- *Imagination is the root of creativity.*
- *Creativity is putting imagination to work.*
- *Innovation is putting new ideas into practice.*[4]

In the simplest of terms, imagination is the ability to generate new or novel ideas. Imagination can stand on its own and live within its own universe. We don't have to see it to know it exists.

To understand creativity, we need to see imagination at work. An artist's creativity is measured through the art he or she produces. We need to hear music to understand what is happening in a musician's imagination. For a mathematician, it might be an elegant mathematical theory. For a medical researcher, it might be a new drug. For an entrepreneur, it might be a new type of business. For an engineer, it might be a mechanical device. We call people creative when we see the imagination in real or physical terms.

Innovation, in many ways, is often a measure of influence or magnitude. How much impact does the creative invention have? Does it invent something entirely new? Does it transform a science or an industry and take it in a new direction? Does it completely displace something that existed before? We call people innovators when the output of their imagination is transformational.

All three are versions of the creative, but all *forms* of creativity start with the imagination. So, let's dig into what it really is and how it works. We'll start at ten thousand feet and work downward.

IT'S NOT WHAT YOU THINK...

When we think of imagination, we often picture a lightning bolt from the sky lighting up our brains. Or perhaps, we take our cue from a thousand different versions of a famous movie scene—a mad scientist shouting Eureka!

But what's really happening?

> **Secret #1:** All of our thoughts and feelings are *representations* in our minds of specific experiences we have had or are having. The *experience* of an "Ah-ha!" moment is the *connection* of two completely separate and previously *unconnected* thoughts or concepts. In most cases, you have put together something in your mind that you simply had not connected before. In some cases, no one you know or work with has connected those dots before. In other cases, no one in the world has connected those dots before. At its very base, *imagination is a new connection.*

I hate to do this to you, but to truly understand how this process works, we're going to take a deeper dive into the brain and the mind. The discussion contains a mix of biology, psychology, and neuroscience. It can get pretty complex, so I will do everything I can to keep it simple and try not to put you to sleep. I would hate to lose you before we get into the really good stuff.

The primary brain concepts I want you to understand by the end of this chapter are *neuroplasticity* and *synaptic pruning*. In the next chapter, I'll give you a brief introduction to the basic *brain anatomy* and *memory*. By the fourth chapter, we will pull this all together to give you a clear picture of the processes and mechanics of what we call imagination.

BUILDING BLOCKS OF THE MIND

Neurons

The building blocks of the brain and the nervous system are neurons, sometimes called nerve cells. They are specialized cells designed to transmit information throughout the body via electrical and chemical signals. Neurons consist of a cell body, dendrites (which receive signals), and an axon (which transmits signals).

Figure 2.1

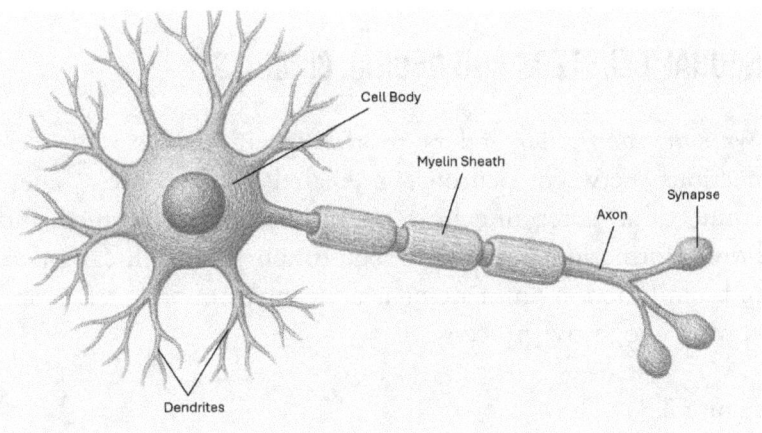

The key functions of neurons are signal transmission, communication with each other through electrical and chemical signals, and information processing, receiving, integrating, and interpreting signals for an appropriate response. They are essential for all brain functions such as thinking, feeling, and learning.

The brain itself is composed mainly of neurons. The neurons are supported by glial cells that provide nutrients, protection, and insulation. The remainder of the brain consists of water, which transports the nutrients and waste; fat, which provides insulation and serves as an energy storage source; and proteins, which are essential for building and maintaining brain cells and performing various functions.

Synapses

Synapses are the *connections* that facilitate communication between two neurons or between a neuron and another cell, like a muscle or gland cell. Synapses are crucial for processes like learning, memory, muscle control, and sensory perception.

NEURAL CLUSTERS AND NEURAL CIRCUITS

Synaptic connectivity refers to the specific pattern of connections between neurons, mediated by synapses. These connections determine how neural circuits are formed and how information flows within the brain. It's a critical aspect of brain function, influencing everything from basic reflexes to complex cognitive processes.

Figure 2.2

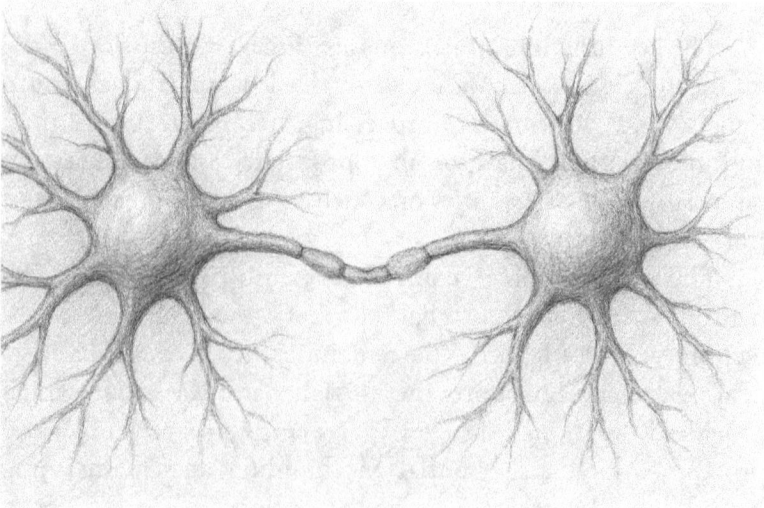

Neural clusters refer to groups of neurons that are connected and fire together, or exhibit similar activity patterns, forming functional units within the nervous system. These clusters can range in size and complexity, from small groups of neurons to larger, more organized structures.

Neural circuits are populations of neurons interconnected by synapses to carry out specific functions when activated. These circuits are fundamental to the nervous system, enabling communication and information processing between different parts of the brain and body. They can range in complexity from simple reflexive arcs (such as a knee-jerk reflex) to elaborate networks underlying complex cognitive behaviors, like recognizing faces. A neural circuit is generally considered a broader and more functional entity, while a neural cluster is a more localized grouping of neurons or synapses within that larger circuit.

Biological neural networks are the highly complex, intricate networks of neurons, potentially connecting to millions or even billions of other neurons.

Figure 2.3

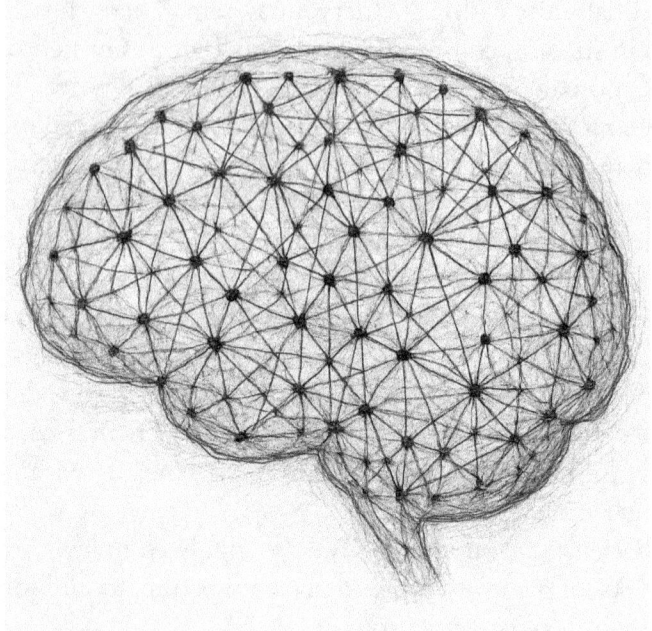

The foundational understanding of how the brain functions is this: Neurons connect and form clusters and circuits, all of which control communication to other parts of the brain and throughout the body. The largest and most complex functions bring together various circuits and form highly complex networks.

NEUROGENESIS

Neurogenesis is the fancy word for the formation of neurons. While it's most active during prenatal development, neurogenesis continues in specific brain regions throughout life. By the age of three, a child's brain has approximately one hundred billion neurons, each with ten thousand possible connections. The number of connections between these neurons, the *synapses*, dramatically increases during the first few years of life, with a toddler's brain having about twice as many synapses as an adult brain. Children have up to one quadrillion brain connections. At a very early age, we have this robust and powerful network available to us.

Neuroplasticity

Neuroplasticity is the brain's capacity to modify its structure and function *in response to experience*. Neuroplasticity is a lifelong process that enables learning, recovery from brain damage, and the formation of new neural pathways and habits.

In his 1949 book, *The Organization of Behavior*, Donald Hebb, a Canadian psychologist known for his work on neuropsychology, introduced what is now known as the Hebbian Theory, or Hebb's Rule:

> *Neurons that fire together, wire together.*

This principle was groundbreaking in its explanation of how learning and memory are formed in the brain. The general idea is that any two cells or systems of cells that are repeatedly active simultaneously will tend to become associated so that activity in one facilitates activity in the other. Basically, repetitive firing creates a stronger connection. Repeated exposure to similar types of experiences creates similar firing patterns, strengthening or expanding specific neural clusters and circuits. Over time, these patterns begin to rewire our brains.

One of my favorite authors on the subject of how our minds work is Dr. Daniel Siegel. He has written numerous books on the subject, including *The Developing Mind* and *The Whole Brain Child*. He is credited as the founder of interpersonal neurobiology and is widely known for his interdisciplinary approach. In his work, Dr. Siegel expands the concept behind the Hebbian theory to the following:

Where attention goes, neurons grow.

Essentially, Dr. Siegel adds *focus* to the equation. "The point is that the physical architecture of the brain changes according to where we direct our attention and what we practice doing… By directing our attention, we can go from being influenced by factors within and around us, to influencing them."[5]

Not only do our brains have the ability to change and grow by establishing new connections and reinforcing old ones, but we also have the ability to influence those changes through experience and through attention. I'll add one more degree to this:

Myelin Sheath (See Figure 2.1)

The myelin sheath is a fatty insulating layer that surrounds the axons of many neurons, enabling faster and more efficient transmission of nerve impulses. It acts like insulation on an electrical wire, preventing signal leakage. The primary function of the myelin sheath is to speed up the transmission of nerve impulses along the axon. The stronger and thicker the myelin sheath, the faster and more efficient the communication is between neurons. The weaker the myelin sheath is, the slower and less efficient the communication is. This impacts all functions of the neurons, including learning, memory, motor skills, and more.

Like the neurons and connections, the myelin itself has plasticity. It can be influenced by neuronal activity and experiences, impacting how neural circuits function. Research indicates that neuronal activity can directly influence myelination (thickening of the myelin sheath). When brain circuits are used frequently, such as when learning a new skill, they can become more myelinated, allowing for faster and more efficient communication within those circuits. Fibers with thicker layers of Myelin can conduct signals as much as 100X faster.

Synaptic pruning

Opposite the process of neurogenesis, and as an integral part of the brain's ability to change, is synaptic pruning. In the first few years of life, nature is busy building us the biggest, most robust brain it can afford so that we have an immense capacity to learn and grow at incredible speed. By age three, the brain begins to prune away unused connections, making the remaining connections more efficient. This happens for the rest of our lives. At the same time, the brain will also experience *demyelination,* the breakdown of our protective coating between our neural circuitries. Those areas, connections, and circuits we do not use will eventually wither away or weaken, and we will lose the capacity to use them.

The brain is a "use it or lose it" organ.

We know that we have the power to influence how connections are formed in our mind, and we also know that we have the power to lose it. Let's look at the broader picture in the following chapter.

Chapter 3

BRAIN ANATOMY AND FUNCTION

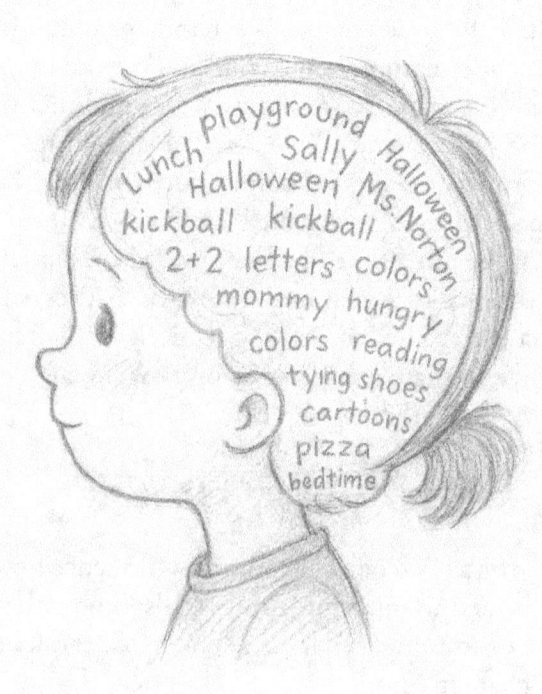

The brain itself is made up of a multitude of areas and functions. It would take me a thousand pages to explain in detail all of the distinct parts, different terms, and specific functions of each area of the brain. Again, our focus is on the unique process of imagination and creativity, so we'll try to focus on what's important.

The brain has three primary areas:

- *Cerebrum.* That's the big fluffy part of the brain we're accustomed to seeing in pictures and movies. It's divided into two hemispheres—commonly referred to as the left and right brain—and four lobes. The *frontal lobe* is the biggest part of the brain and sits primarily in your forehead above your eyes. The *parietal lobe* sits at the top of your head, just behind the frontal lobe. The *occipital lobe* sits at the back of the brain. There are two *temporal lobes*, each located on the side of the brain just above your ears and around your temples.

  The cerebrum performs higher-level cognitive functions such as thinking, reasoning and problem solving, learning, and memory. It processes sensory information, such as touch, vision, and hearing. It processes language and emotions.

- *Cerebellum.* Just below the cerebrum, at the very back of the brain, is a smaller structure that half-circles the brainstem. The cerebellum is responsible for coordination and balance.
- *Brainstem.* Below the cerebrum and in front of the cerebellum is the brainstem. It connects the brain to the spinal cord and is essential for basic life functions, such as breathing, heart rate, and blood pressure, as well as

automatic functions, such as swallowing, digestion, and sneezing.

Other important parts of the brain include:

Prefrontal Cortex. Essential for executive functions, including working memory, attention, impulse control, and planning. Involved in making complex decisions, weighing potential outcomes, and reasoning through problems. Helps us understand social cues, regulate emotions, and make appropriate social decisions. Modulates emotional responses, helping us manage fear, anxiety, and other emotions.

The Limbic System is a network of interconnected brain structures that play a crucial role in emotions, memory, and motivation. The main parts of the limbic system include:

- *Hippocampus:* Involved in the formation of new memories (especially episodic and spatial memory) and their consolidation.
- *Amygdala*: Processes emotions like fear, anxiety, pleasure, and anger. It also plays a key role in attaching emotional significance to memories.
- *Hypothalamus*: Regulates homeostatic functions like hunger, thirst, sleep, body temperature, and circadian rhythms. It also plays a crucial role in sexual behavior, maternal bonding, and aggression. The hypothalamus is the primary output relay for the limbic system, connecting with the autonomic nervous system and the endocrine system.
- *Thalamus:* Serves as a relay station for sensory and motor signals, filtering and processing information before sending it to the cerebral cortex.
- *Corpus Callosum.* A large band of nerve fibers connecting the left and right cerebral hemispheres of the

brain. It plays a crucial role in interhemispheric communication, enabling coordination and integration of functions between the two sides of the brain.

Do we need to know or memorize all of these different areas to understand the imagination? No. Just an understanding of how the brain functions. The brain is composed of a series of layered pathways and connections. Different areas of the brain perform different tasks and can be responsible for specific functions. What is more important to understand is that the *majority of human functions are interconnected*. Most often, our brain operates with multiple regions and areas working together. Information and its transition are the key to coordination, which is why the neural circuitry plays such an important role. Here are some examples of interconnected brain coordination:

Voluntary movement involves the frontal lobe for initiation, the cerebellum for coordination and balance, and various areas in the motor cortex for planning and execution.

Language involves different areas for speech production and comprehension, and other areas for word association and emotional content.

Even something as simple as *eating* involves the hypothalamus, the brainstem, the amygdala, the hippocampus, and the prefrontal cortex.

The more complex the function, the more areas of the brain that are involved. And as you will see later in this chapter, *imagination is the most complex process of all*. I want to emphasize the importance of integration.

Dr. Siegel's book *The Whole-Brain Child* spends a lot of time on the integrated aspect of the brain. He sets a framework of the brain into the upper, lower, left, and right parts. In general, the brain transitions from more instinctual functions, such as survival, to higher reasoning functions, including planning and interpreting, as we move from the lower parts of the brain, like the amygdala, to the higher parts, such as the prefrontal cortex. He describes how the right and left parts of the brain work together to integrate aspects like logic and emotion. A primary thesis of this book is that the better a child has integrated the various parts of the brain, the stronger and healthier the child's mental health will be. Dr. Siegel advocates strongly for both vertical and horizontal integration of the brain's individual parts. It's essential to note that the goal is not to assimilate all areas of the brain, but to enhance their ability and efficiency to work together.

I found these insights both highly correlated with and deeply encouraging for this book. Much of the work done with the imagination requires a highly integrated mind. Efforts to build and maintain highly efficient neural networks not only can make us more imaginative and creative, but they also make us mentally healthy. Now that we have laid down some of the basic brain parts, let's talk about how it actually functions.

MEMORY

Our memory is an integral part of our ability to be creative. Imagination and creativity are connected to the storage and recall of information within our minds. When most of us think of memory, we imagine a sort of photo album or filing cabinet, where images are neatly stored away and labeled for future reference. Have you ever wondered why some things are much harder to remember than others? Have you ever wondered why we can forget something we did yesterday, but remember crashing our bike when we were six years old in vivid detail?

Memory is much more complex than we imagine. The brain is an amazing machine that constantly reads the room, interprets the information, and responds accordingly. Take something as simple as walking down the street. Your brain reads *everything*. On your left, it sees the glass windows of the shops and records the different products being sold in each one. It sees the sidewalk underneath your feet and lets you know to avoid stepping off the curb. A woman passes by and smiles. Your brain records the sex of the person, the color of her hair, the clothes she is wearing, the expression on her face, and tells you to respond with a pleasant smile. It notices the parked cars on your left and checks to see if the meters are paid. As you move to cross to the other side, it reminds you to look left, then right, then back again for your own safety. While in the middle of the street, it notices the couple you are approaching and attempts to listen in on the conversation. You sense tension, so it seems like an argument of some sort. As you continue forward, your brain records that the shops are now on your right and the street is on your left. A car passes with its radio blaring. It's a seventies song you haven't heard in years.

All of this happens in real time, but your memory is working in three dimensions. It's looking at the past, present, and future all at once. It's not only taking in input, it's also providing you with output. When it's recording, it's not just filing away sequential images; it's associating your *current experience* with a whole host of *past experiences,* providing you with context, then anticipating what could happen in your next few steps. So how does it work?

YOUR MEMORY WORKS IN THREE DIMENSIONS: THE PAST, PRESENT, AND FUTURE.

The brain is a combination of wiring (our previously discussed neural circuits) and associations, as well as how and where our memories are stored. It takes in a host of internal and external stimuli—sights, sounds, touch, feelings, people, environment, circumstances, emotion—bounces them off its memories and gathered knowledge for context, and decides where this new information should be recorded and for what purpose. For example, as you walk down the street, it knows both where you are going and for what purpose; two vital pieces of information in its decision-making. It also decides whether each person approaching is a threat. This is an endless loop of interaction and reaction.

As we discussed earlier, experiences aren't stored in one place. Sight, for example, is stored in the occipital lobe. At the same time, sound is recorded in the auditory cortex; smell in the olfactory cortex; taste in the gustatory cortex; and touch in the somatosensory cortex located in the parietal lobes. Walking, as another example, requires motor memory. Motor memory is stored in the cerebellum, which coordinates fine motor movement; the basal ganglia, which helps plan motor action; the hippocampus, which stores facts and events; the prefrontal cortex, which processes decision-making and coordination; and the motor cortex, which controls voluntary movements.

It's important to note that there are different types of memories:

Implicit memory—a form of long-term memory expressed unconsciously and without deliberate effort, influencing our behaviors, skills, and emotional responses without us being aware of it.

Explicit memory involves the conscious recollection of facts and events. It's the type of memory we use when we intentionally try to recall something, such as a specific event or a piece of information.

Short-term memory vs. *long-term memory*—distinct types of memory with different durations and capacities. Short-term memory, also known as working memory, holds information temporarily, typically for seconds to minutes, while long-term memory can store information for more extended periods, potentially years.

MENTAL MAPS

What does all of this memory have to do with imagination and creativity? Memory involves four distinct processes: gathering the information, encoding the information, storing the information, and retrieving the information. Because information isn't stored in a single place, memory and imagination rely on the coordinated efforts of neurons and *circuits to* find the information they need. Hence, the importance of strong neural networks and *connections* we discussed earlier. And just as important is a process we'll refer to as *Assembly,* where the brain retrieves the information, puts it back together in some form, and presents it back to you with context.

Roads, Bridges, and Highways…

In 1850, there were essentially two primary ways to travel between New York and San Francisco, but each had variations that could be considered different routes:

1. Sea Routes: Those looking to make the trip could travel by boat. At the time, there were three routes: Around Cape Horn, through the isthmus of Panama, or through Nicaragua. Both Panama and Nicaragua required short distances by land as part of the journey.
2. Overland Routes: Travelers could use the Northern Route, following the Missouri River through Montana and the Oregon territory; the Southern Route, traveling through St. Louis and Memphis, traversing Texas, New Mexico, Arizona, and California; and the California Trail, following the Platte River and crossing the southern pass in Wyoming.

Options were limited to a scarce few, all dangerous, long, and complex. Today, we have thousands of choices. JFK, LaGuardia, and Newark airports offer something like two thousand possible direct flights per week. There are multiple train routes with transfers in places like Chicago. Travelers can take at least twenty different bus routes on a Greyhound. The number of routes by car is practically unlimited, depending on where you decide to stop or how scenic you want the trip to be. The vast network of roads and highways provides a reasonable estimate of at least one hundred thousand options.

Because our brain is an integrated network of pathways and connections, one way to think about its construction is a system of roads, bridges, and highways. Later on, you will hear me refer to this as *Access*. To optimize both our memory processes and our imagination, we need fast and efficient access to all of the varied parts of the brain and its stored information.

This requires fast, robust networks. As highlighted by the travel routes from New York to San Francisco, imagine your brain as the available network in the 1850s. The pathways between important functions are limited, difficult to traverse, and poorly traveled. Each journey between two sites is long and unsure. Now imagine those same journeys today. The choices are unlimited; we can reach our destination in multiple ways. We can take scenic routes and see beautiful new places we've never seen before, or we can jump on a plane and get there as quickly as possible.

Due to our brains' *neuroplasticity*, we can impact the number of pathways and connections, but we can also influence the size, strength, and speed of those connections. Our goal is to go from a few tired, grassy foot trails to a head full of superhighways with millions of alternative routes.

CASTLES AND KEEPS

Not all information is stored equally. Csikszentmihalyi discusses this extensively in *Flow*:

> An individual can only experience so much. Therefore, the information we allow into consciousness becomes extremely important... While everything we feel, smell, hear, and remember is potentially a candidate for entering consciousness, the experiences that actually do become a part of it are much fewer than those left out. Thus, while consciousness is a mirror that reflects what our senses tell us about what happens both outside our bodies and within the nervous system, it reflects those changes selectively, actively shaping events, imposing on them a reality of its own. The reflection consciousness provides is what we call our life: The sum of all we have heard, seen, felt, hoped, and suffered from birth to death... These principles include how sensory data are processed, stored, and used, the dynamics of attention and memory.[6]

The brain's short-term and long-term capacities and its ability to draw on those memories are limited, so the brain prioritizes certain pieces of information over others. Csikszentmihalyi uses an analogy of passing cars: If you walked for about twenty minutes on a very busy street, hundreds of cars would likely pass you. The brain sees everything through the eyes and hears through the ears, but it doesn't necessarily encode each and every car in a place that is meant to be immediately accessible or usable. It simply registers "car" as it passes by and maybe alerts your system to avoid being hit. However, if a dog on a leash rushes you and barks loudly, making you jump for a second, that memory is likely to be recorded and more easily recalled. If a stray dog actually bites you, sending you to the hospital for eighteen stitches and a rabies shot, it is an experience you will remember and be able to recall for the rest of your life. Emotion, as an example, is a huge driver of robust memory. We all remember our first kiss. So is pain. We all remember that first breakup. The power of an experience helps us hardcode memories into accessible pathways, connections, and associations.

The brain decides the *relevancy* and *importance* of millions of bits of information and where to file them away. When searching for original ideas, the bit of information that finally makes a new connection might be hidden away from plain sight.

> **EMOTION IS A HUGE DRIVER OF ROBUST MEMORY.**

When you add the process of synaptic pruning to the equation, over time, you begin to lose pathways and bridges to much of that information. Connections to poorly used areas of the brain and memory begin to disappear, leaving behind forgotten lands and castles in the mind. The most distant memories and thoughts can get locked away behind the drawbridge in castle keeps or lost in dark caves. Entire books are written on the concepts of unlocking the mind; we need to access those ideas.

MAPS AND DIRECTIONS

That brain, that mind, that thing inside our head we all believe controls and manages our thoughts and actions, is a giant MAZE of connections. Everything you think and feel is based on these connections. Only your brain knows where to store everything. Therefore, it's likely the only one who knows how to retrieve it. To do so, the brain uses a series of patterns and associations to draw its own maps. Frequently-used information sits on well-traveled highways and is easy to get directions to. That's what you experience when driving home at night; it's not difficult because you do it every day. Rare or little-used information sits on isolated islands and in dark forests, making it much more difficult to describe, let alone find. That's what you experience when someone on the street says hello, and you remember them from somewhere, but you can't recall their name. Hours later, it suddenly hits you that you attended elementary school together, but hadn't seen each other in many years. The brain remembers—it just took a while to find the correct associations.

The art of assembly

The output process of memory is to retrieve different bits of information, decipher them, and *assemble* them in a way that's understandable. It does so using its own maps and patterns. These mental maps contain guidance and direction and help us put together usable information in a fast and efficient way.

According to Dr. Siegel, part of the brain's job is to integrate our implicit and explicit memory:

> The hippocampus works with the different parts of our brains to take all the images, emotions, and sensations of implicit memories and draw them together so they can become the assembled pictures that make up our understanding of our past.[7]

It's these assembled pictures that give us our understanding of everything. Assembly is the key to our ability to imagine.

To better understand the full picture, I need to mention one final aspect of memory.

The neuronal ensemble

I believe I first came across the concept in a TED Talk by Andrey Vyshedskiy, a PhD in neuroscience from Boston University, titled "The Science of Imagination." Neuronal ensembles are groups of neurons that exhibit coordinated activity patterns and are thought to be fundamental building blocks of neural circuits. They are considered functional units involved in various brain processes, including memory, perception, and motor control. These ensembles can be activated spontaneously or by specific stimuli, and their activity is remarkably stable across different contexts.[8]

For example, the concept of a "car" can be tied to multiple experiences encoded as *associations* in various locations throughout the brain. When you ask your brain for an image of a car, it might recall multiple experiences at once. The retrieved information could look something like this:

> wheels—door handles—red—wind—"Don't Stop Believing" by Journey—my little sister—the family trip to Florida in 1993—glovebox—the fender bender near Roland's house—my first speeding ticket—car—leather seats—my first—tires squealing—the window rolled down—2012 Chevy Camaro—Christmas at Grandma's house

If this is how information was presented back to us, we would all be confused all the time. That's where the brain's ability to *associate* and *assemble* comes in to help us *construct* the ideas that become our thoughts, feelings, and actions.

Chapter 4

THE *REAL* PROCESS OF IMAGINATION

The process of how random and seemingly disconnected ideas are eventually connected is one of the most complex processes known to science. Why? Because using the imagination requires tapping into all the brain's encoded information, making the connection between two dots that have never been connected before takes us into uncharted territory. There are likely no roads, no bridges, and no map to tell us how to get there. Important pieces of information could be tucked away in places that haven't been accessed for years. So, in many cases, we might have to construct and connect our way there.

I am going to demystify the process for you.

Your brain is built to do whatever you ask of it. If it could fulfill all your wildest dreams and requests, it would. In its simplest form, the brain takes in your request and uses all of its power and capabilities to provide you with an adequate response. When you do even the most basic tasks, you are asking it to *do* something.

Hey, Brain, can you comb my hair?

Hey, Brain, can you remind me to set the alarm?

Hey, Brain, what's that actor's name on my favorite show?

Hey, Brain, let's put my roller skates on and skate down the hill?

Hey, Brain, will you help me finish my math homework?

When we speak about the imagination, we follow the same process. We are asking the brain to come up with a new idea, process, invention, concept, or whatever. The brain, in response, immediately sifts through all its known information, traveling all the familiar pathways in your brain, pulling together associations, and hoping its answer will be sufficient. It reads through every fact, feeling, memory, and experience we have ever known right up until the minute you asked the question. If it doesn't get it right, it will try again, this time going down less-traveled pathways and coming up with different associations.

A monkey and a beer? Nope.

A fish and a tractor? Nope.

Peanut butter and mayonnaise? Not for me!

Shorts at a wedding? Please don't.

Chocolate and bacon? You had me at Hello.

The brain will literally do this as many times as you ask it until it is exhausted and completely out of options. The diagram below provides an example of what really happens when the brain is searching for an original connection.

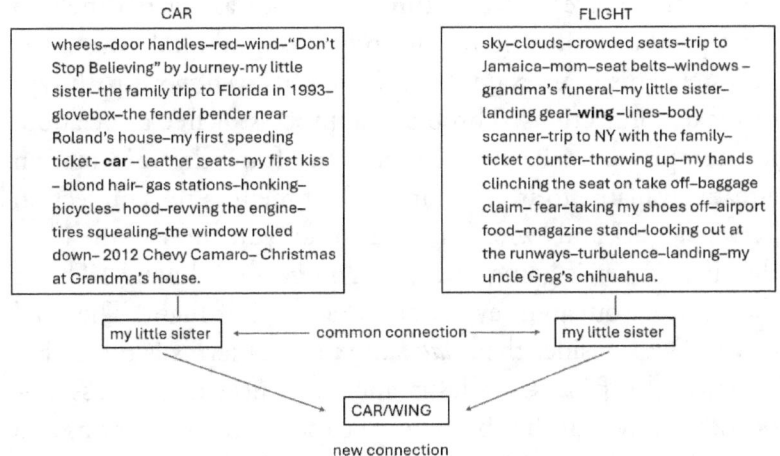

Let's start with the example I gave above, using the brain's concept and associations around "car." Since you were a little kid, you have been fascinated by the idea of a flying car. The idea has been around for more than one hundred years, so you don't understand why no one has figured it out yet. You've seen it on *The Jetsons*. You ask your brain to come up with some way that cars can fly.

The easier pathways are often emotionally connected, frequently involving positive memories and traumatic events. Physical items are easily recalled. People we frequently talk to or hold dear. The more difficult an idea is to find, the more it moves away from easy-to-find information and begins to search for uncommon and infrequent associations. It's within this process of *free association* that we find new connections. Eventually, one of these new connections is useful in some way to us. The best ones lead us *toward* the idea we are looking for. And finally, the right connection becomes the "ah-ha!" moment. It's that simple, and it's that difficult all at the same time.

In the example above, the brain files through everything it can find associated with cars and the concept of flight. In your brain's current architecture, it has not associated the two concepts, but in its research, it finds a common link—your little sister. This is an example of it using its well-worn pathways to make connections. Through the process of free association, it attempts to make new connections from the information already available to it. The "ah-ha!" moment is the connection between "car" and "wing". In your head, you connect the ideas that if your car is going to fly, it's going to need wings. This is the start of your journey toward a new era of flight. The total of what we consider the *imagination* in real terms is the ability to repeat this process endlessly and come up with new associations. Creativity is the ability to take these new associations and apply them to something we are trying to build or understand.

As we have discussed earlier, the fewer the pathways, the fewer the options. The fewer the experiences, the fewer the options. The fewer the bits of information scattered throughout the mind, the fewer the options. All our ability to associate is predicated on how we have wired our brains, and the way our brains are wired is based on experiences. The object of the game is to create *experiences* that foster *connections,* allowing for rapid *associations*.

It's not that you are not creative; it's that you are out of practice. You are not in tune with the process of imagination. You haven't mastered the skills, you haven't built the muscles, and you haven't done the work. The following chapter is dedicated to showing you how to master the *process* of imagination. Before we get started, we need to talk about a few more things related to the brain and its functions.

DEFAULT MODE AND FLOW

The conscious and the subconscious

The majority of us have an idea of what these two terms represent. In general terms, the conscious mind is the active mind, the one we are aware of, the one we are always using to run our day, make decisions, and guide our thinking. The subconscious mind lies somewhere underneath. It does things we are not always aware of, it holds secrets, and runs wild when we are asleep at night. While both images are oversimplifications, they are adequate for our understanding of the two primary states of mind: sort of Active and Inactive. That is, what your brain does when it's wide awake and managing your participation in the world, and what it's doing when you have shut out the lights and disconnected from the day's requirements.

To avoid spending chapters on the differences and aspects of the extremely complex conscious and subconscious minds, we'll focus on two concepts that drive our ability to imagine and create: Default Mode and Flow.

Default mode

Default mode could be described as perhaps the deepest form of the subconscious. Think of default mode as the period when the active mind shuts down and quieter, mind-wandering takes over. Neuroscience and modern brain imaging have shown that when the task-oriented mind, known as the Dorsal Attention Network (DAN), shuts down, a network of brain areas called the Default Mode Network (DMN) takes over or lights up. It's in this state that the brain exhibits its greatest capacity for free association and "mind-wandering." When in default mode, the brain can explore novel thoughts and ideas without the interference and constraints of our more linear, organized, and biased thought patterns. This state allows it to test and consider connections between seemingly unrelated ideas, the very foundation of imagination. It also actively integrates both internal and external information and experiences into novel combinations.

Mihaly Csikszentmihalyi talks about the power of this subconscious state in his book *Creativity*:

> Cognitive theorists believe that ideas, when deprived of conscious direction, follow simple laws of association… Intentionality does not work in the subconscious. Free from rational direction, ideas can combine and pursue every which way. Because of this freedom, original connections that would be first rejected by the rational mind have a chance to become established… Incubation… seems to occur within the mind's hidden recesses where consciousness is unable to reach.[9]

Flow

Flow, on the other hand, can be described as one of the higher states of consciousness. It is the ultimate focus on the task at hand. Csikszentmihalyi's book, *Flow,* most appropriately describes the ideas and process of deep focus. The thoughts and concepts in this book have been highly influential on my own thoughts as well as others. What I absolutely love about the underlying science is that the book is actually a search for higher states of happiness. Csikszentmihalyi describes flow as having eight essential components:

1. A challenging activity that requires skill.
2. Merging action and awareness.
3. Clear goals.
4. Immediate feedback.
5. Deep, effortless involvement that removes the worries and frustrations of everyday life.
6. A sense of control over our actions.
7. The disappearance of self-concern.
8. The alteration or absence of time.

Like within default mode, much of our conditioned and ordered world tends to fade into the background. During flow, the focus is so intense we lose track of time, ourselves, our worries, and our fears. The brain is solely focused on the task at hand and the pursuit of its achievement. The result is freedom of thought and action that is nonexistent in lesser states of consciousness. For me, flow moves beyond just happiness and enters the realm of human potential. In the next chapter, I will discuss how integral flow is in the development of creativity, achievement, and mental health.

Many people believe these two states are mutually exclusive, and the brain only holds so much capacity and energy to accomplish what we ask of it. That's why Csikszentmihalyi has spent so much time focused on the idea of *attention*. It's true that while one state is active, the other is suppressed, but other studies have shown that the brain has the capacity to work in the background.

There is a third powerful state I like to call the *passive* state. Dr. Siegel describes one aspect of intrinsic memory as the ability to perform tasks without much effort, as the sequencing or "memory" associated with performing this task is hardwired into our circuitry. A perfect example of this would be walking. By the time we are out of the toddler phase, most of us can walk without having to think or remember a set of instructions such as "put one foot in front of the other, that's good, now the left, now the right." We've done it enough times so that it's automatic. When we are performing automatic tasks, the brain is following instructions and requires minimal effort and energy. The remaining capacity for thinking can actually be used for other things at the same time. This is what I refer to as a passive state because it's not completely active or inactive from a mental perspective. All of us are familiar with "daydreaming" while doing simple, repetitive tasks. That's because part of the mind is occupied while part of it is free. That brings me to the next secret of the imagination.

> **SECRET #2:** The highest states of imagination don't occur in default mode. Imagination is most productive in what I like to call "Twilight Mode," a state located just between the conscious and the subconscious.

TWILIGHT MODE

> *Alice laughed. "There's no use trying," she said. "One can't believe impossible things."*
>
> *"I dare say you haven't had much practice," said the Queen. "When I was your age, I always did it for half-an-hour a day. Why, sometimes I've believed as many as six impossible things before breakfast."*
>
> —Lewis Carroll, author of *Alice's Adventures in Wonderland*

Six impossible things before breakfast—absolutely one of my favorite quotes. Have you ever had a dream that is so bizarre you wake up thinking to yourself, "What on earth?" You turn to your spouse immediately and wake them up:

> Honey, I have to tell you this story. I'm riding an ostrich up a mountain slope. It was either in Turkey or Argentina, I couldn't tell. As I'm going along, a shaman approaches and offers to sell me beans in exchange for the last known timepiece on earth. I tell him I don't have one, but he makes me look into the satchel on my ostrich, and sure enough, it's there. I give it to him, and I ask what the beans do. He says, "Nothing," and starts laughing at me. The hoodie over his head slips down behind, revealing my uncle Ralph. He walks away and just keeps shouting, "I'm out of time, I'm out of time." I look down, and the ostrich is gone, but I'm being led away by a monkey.

Default mode is awesome! It's the most powerful place in which our brains practice free association. But wandering the cosmos of our minds can produce some pretty crazy results. It's what I like to call the wild frontier. It is magic for pushing the limits of exploration and dreaming. But I'm going to give you a better magic trick for the connection of usable ideas. I'll share it in the form of my morning routine.

Morning Routine

Each morning, I rise around four thirty a.m. Not because I am chasing the proverbial worm like the early bird. But because it's quiet. There is no noise and no demands on my time. I haven't yet entered the bustle of the day, where my thoughts and actions can be interrupted by any one of a thousand problems or requests to occupy my time and energy.

It's just me and my thoughts.

I wake up, make myself a cup of coffee, and sit in darkness for thirty minutes to one hour. It is the greatest form of meditation I have experienced.

I find this time the closest to being the perfect moment for creativity. I have just woken up and exited a long-running default mode where my mind was free to roam for hours. I'm not quite awake, so my conscious mind hasn't fully kicked in. I float in and out of conscious thinking, or *twilight mode*. The coffee keeps me from falling completely back asleep.

My mind is still full of random thoughts, but it is reaching for the conscious. It is within these moments that the greatest connections take place. On most days, I cannot contain ideas. I sit there until my mind is so active that it makes me get up and write down what is coming out. This may last for ten minutes or an hour.

When the initial blast fades, I generally take a shower—another great way to slide into twilight mode. Again, I am slowly waking my mind to the conscious while staying calm and relaxed. This routine usually produces a second round of thoughts, and I find myself bouncing out of the shower, dying to write down these new ideas.

From there, I get dressed and attempt to stay in the mode, often with the pen and paper, sometimes the computer, but I stick with it until all of the creative energy has been worked out. Sometimes this dies quickly; other days, I can stay focused for hours.

Once this round has lost its fuel, I offer a third. I go for a walk. I do not turn on the phone or listen to music. I want my mind free to roam. Once again, much of what was rolling around in my head resurfaces, or, often now, trails of thought. I'm in a *passive state*, trying to reconnect with *twilight mode*. I keep paper and pen with me on my walk to write down whatever diatribe comes out. I am not afraid to stop and let it spill out.

While this may seem like an extravagant routine for a busy life, you might be surprised to know that, on most mornings, this outburst ends by eight a.m. Because I am fully functioning in this mode by five a.m. I get at least three hours of twilight mode before most people have coffee.

Twilight mode allows us to use the incredible power of free association and connect it with the real world. It's like all the great allegories of traveling into a dark cave and coming out with a new form of truth. We wander into our subconscious and bring something entirely new and original into the conscious. People have been searching for the power of *twilight mode* for centuries. It was often the work of the shaman, or the medicine man. Cultures have produced sophisticated rituals to induce this state. Artists and musicians have sometimes turned to hallucinogens in search of the *muse*. This is completely unnecessary. We already have the power to induce states of daydreaming. You can travel in your mind as deep as you want to go. You just have to know the path and the tools.

DEFAULT SETTINGS

Something even more powerful happens with this morning routine. This creative burst is so powerful, my mind searches for it the rest of the day. As I go about the rest of life's responsibilities and pressures, my subconscious continues working in the background. My brain can't wait to return to default mode, and throughout the day, I often find myself drifting away from my responsibilities and returning to random thoughts.

In general, I try to juice this entire process with input—reading and prompts, which I'll discuss later in the book. I usually drift off to sleep at night with my mind searching for some form of answer to a question I've proposed, or an idea I'm working on. My mind moves from the conscious back into the subconscious, slowly, and eventually, I'm deep back into default mode where the wild rumpus begins.

> **MY DEFAULT SETTING IS DAYDREAMING.**

When people say, "You are so creative," or "I don't know how you come up with so many ideas," it's because I've trained my mind to stay in this mode as much as humanly possible. Whenever I have five minutes of silence, my brain immediately resets to some form of twilight mode or daydreaming. If I had to express one of the most important messages in this entire book, it would be this: People with powerful creative instincts and huge imaginations all have this quality. Their factory reset is default mode. Over many years, they have developed a series of habits, exercises, and routines, whether consciously or subconsciously, that return them to this frame of mind. They simply spend way more time daydreaming than the average person.

What is your default setting?

Our brains, in general, aren't accustomed to silence. Unfortunately, for many of us, if we have five minutes of unoccupied time, our minds immediately turn to problems, issues, or tasks we need to do, like stopping by the grocery store. In many ways, we have trained our brain to use downtime to focus on worries. It's part of why we have such high rates of anxiety and depression. Because no one *likes* to spend their time worrying, we have adopted most of our responses by practicing *avoidance*.

We would rather do anything than worry. So we turn to distractions like television, alcohol, gossip, hobbies, and so on. The worst thing that has happened to society in the last twenty years is our addiction to cell phones. Be honest, you are likely guilty of having that affliction. You are not alone. All you have to do is look around any restaurant, your work, walking down the street, the movie theater, public transportation, in school, or at your own dinner table. Almost everyone who has five minutes to spare immediately turns to their cell phone for entertainment and connection out of boredom. By doing so, we are *training* our minds to seek weak, fast dopamine hits because we are so uncomfortable with silence and letting our minds roam.

What about your child? What is their default setting?

I can help you reset your defaults. Together, we can hardwire your child's default settings to explore and imagine rather than being stuck in the prison of addictive avoidance and distraction. Follow me into the next two chapters.

THE SOCIAL BRAIN

One last comment before we leave the brain. Our brains are entirely social. In Dr. Siegel's words, self and community are interrelated:

> The problem with the single skull perspective—where we consider each individual brain as a lone organ isolated in a single skull, is that it neglects the truth that scientists have come to understand over the last few decades is that the brain is a social organ, made to be in relationship. It's hardwired to take in signals from the social environment, which in turn influences a person's inner world.[10]

This involves both the brain's physical development and our mental health. The brain doesn't develop in isolation. It develops in response to all stimuli, both internal and external. It perceives, it learns from, it reacts to, and it mimics the world and people around us. Like with every other part of the brain, there are thousands of connections related to the external environment. Development without sufficient external and social interaction creates an unbalanced and incomplete mind.

I'll give you an oversimplified example: Imagine a small girl who, one day, sees a tennis champion like Serena Williams and dreams of becoming a tennis star. As she develops, her entire tennis experience has been to play on a half-wall based on a manual she read. She's never spoken with other players, never worked with a coach, never been tested by another player firing shots back over the net, never even played on a full court. She might be an amazing tennis player in her own mind, but what about in reality?

What happens when she faces an opponent for the first time? What happens when a ball zips by at one hundred miles per hour? What happens when her reaction times are too slow? What happens when she is unable to place a single ball within the lines of the opposite court because her spatial perceptions are way off? What happens to her mentally when she drops the first match? The first set? What about when she steps out and faces the pressure of playing in front of others? Can she even step onto the court? It's not her fault that she is not a great tennis player. Everything about her game, from her timing to her speed, instincts, reactions, and mental toughness, is underdeveloped.

> **CHILDREN DEPRIVED OF SOCIAL INTERACTION CAN EXPERIENCE SIGNIFICANT DEVELOPMENTAL DELAYS, INCLUDING COGNITIVE, EMOTIONAL, AND SOCIAL CHALLENGES.**

There are much BIGGER repercussions than a poorly played tennis game. Children deprived of social interaction can experience significant developmental delays, including cognitive, emotional, and social challenges. Lack of social interaction can hinder the development of essential skills like language, communication, and social behavior, potentially leading to issues like anxiety, depression, and low self-esteem. The brain does not properly develop without social interaction. Human beings are not meant to grow in isolation.

As we discuss building strong creative human beings, the building of strong social connections and capabilities is essential to the preservation of humanity. I discuss the need to incorporate social interaction into all our processes extensively in the next two chapters.

SUMMARY

If you're still with me, I appreciate your commitment. I consider the last three chapters the most challenging part of this conversation. If I haven't lost you or put you to sleep at this point, the rest should be downhill. Let's recap before moving on to the fun part.

- Creativity and innovation are practical outcomes of vivid imaginations.
- Imagination is the process of connecting two previously unconnected ideas.
- The brain is an intricate web of connections and circuits.
- We have the power to influence how and where these connections are built.
- The brain operates under a "use it or lose it" principle, and we lose connections over time if they are not used.
- The brain has a sophisticated process of receiving and encoding bits of information in the form of images, facts, emotions, and experiences. It stores these bits of information in many different areas of the brain. These stored images make up what we call knowledge and represent our experience of life.
- The brain uses mental maps and established connections to retrieve this information, assembling it and giving it back to us as organized thought.
- Imagination is the most complex process the brain performs. It utilizes all existing knowledge and experiences and attempts to assemble new ideas through free association and establishing new connections.
- Our brain operates in different states and modes.

- The highest form of imagination resides in a *Twilight Mode* between the conscious and the subconscious. We can create patterns and habits to tap into this creative mode at will.
- The brain is social. All of us require social interaction to fully develop the brain and its attributes.

Chapter 5

THE CAPTAIN OF OUR OWN SHIP

The moment you doubt whether you can fly,
you cease forever to be able to do it.

—J. M. Barrie, author of *Peter Pan*

In 1968, NASA contacted Dr. George Land, author and systems scientist, along with his associate Dr. Beth Jarman, to measure the creative potential of rocket scientists and engineers and identify the most innovative members. Not long after their original test was developed, Land and Jarman conducted a research study on more than sixteen hundred children in the Head Start program between the ages of four and five. The results of the initial study both surprised and confounded them. The original group of participants had scores of 98 percent for what Land and Jarman described as a *genius* level of creativity.

The results were so intriguing that they decided to follow these children in a longitudinal study and see what would happen. They tested these children again when they reached ten years old, fifteen years old, and finally as adults. The results were even more confusing.

By the age of ten, the scores for genius level dropped to only 30 percent.

By the age of fifteen, the scores for genius level dropped to 12 percent.

By the time these children reached adulthood, that number fell to 2 percent.

Many people who have read or heard of the study are stunned at the results. Some have tried to debunk the research, but many others have been able to validate it. I remember the first time I read about it. My reaction? Yeah, that's about right. I had been arguing this for years.

So what happened?

Most fingers get pointed at schools. In many ways, it's an appropriate direction to look in, but I'd like to share a broader perspective. This leads us to Secret #3.

> **SECRET #3:** We kill creativity in most children before the age of ten.
>
> The incredible shift in the loss of creativity between the ages of five and ten years old is a dramatic convergence of three things.
>
> 1. Adults stop playing with children.
> 2. Yes, schools kill creativity.
> 3. Nature helps along the way.

We'll take this one at a time.

First, as adults, we fail their imaginations. "What is that you say? How dare you!" Let me explain. When our children are born, especially with the first one, we are hyper fun. The first five years of a child's life are filled with kisses, hugs, fun, and play. (In this book, I am not addressing the deficits created by either abuse or neglect. I am referring to what might be described as a "typical" childhood.) During this time, we generally do a great job of creating an environment where creativity can blossom. We play peek-a-boo, we buzz their belly buttons with our lips, we toss them in the air. Their rooms and clothes are full of bright colors. All of the toys and items surrounding them are designed for interaction and exploration.

As they get a little older, we play games with them. We chase them down the hall and make monster noises. We roll around and wrestle on the floor. We tell them big, giant, wonderful stories full of imagination and read to them at night. In fact, every relative or friend who comes over comes to play. We are all in on it.

Then something really weird happens. Almost all at once, we stop being fun. We grow tired. We stop playing. From the time they hit kindergarten, our own attitude toward their childhood changes. We let them know that the Easter Bunny and Santa Claus aren't real. We ship them off to someone else's care for much of the day, so we can work at jobs or get stuff done for the family. We begin to focus on or obsess over their ability to perform at school. We start to view them as little adults and ask them to behave accordingly. We spend less and less time making silly noises, showering them with the garden hose, and having imaginary tea parties. It happens at different times for every child, but it happens to all of us.

Second, we tie them to a chair and a desk and take away their natural freedom. I know that sounds a bit dramatic, but children were never meant to spend eight hours indoors, sitting at a desk, preparing for and taking tests. The model designed to create productive factory workers for the Industrial Revolution has been devastating to creativity and imagination. (More on this in chapter 6.)

Third, we do the first two things at the very time our natural biology goes through its own transformation. As we discussed in the previous chapter, by the age of five, 90 percent of the brain's development is complete. The brain has over one hundred billion neurons, each with ten thousand connections. In order to increase efficiency, the brain begins a brutal process of pruning down these connections to focus on the ones we will use consistently. This begins as the entire system is being built in the toddler years. By the age of ten, more than 50 percent of the original connections have been eliminated. The brain "locks in" areas of specialized networks based on what it believes we will need and increases myelination between those connections.

It's no coincidence that as we settle children into a more sedentary lifestyle and draw their *attention* to the processes of learning facts and figures for the purpose of testing, we lose the majority of our ability to imagine. We are literally instructing our brain to prune away these capabilities and *connections* by telling it that they are not important enough to maintain. Due to our focus, we are building pathways dedicated to mindless memorization and not building pathways that would be associated with free association and creativity.

Once we pass the age of ten, the trajectory is set. It's all but determined by then. It's no surprise the trend continues through adolescence, so by the time we reach adulthood, it's pretty much dead. In fact, I don't know how anyone comes out with their imagination intact. We spend twelve to sixteen years placing children into tighter and tighter boxes, and the minute they get out into the real world, we ask them to "think outside the box." At a very early age, we essentially shut down childhood and focus all of our attention on becoming adults.

SELF-HELP

According to Grand View Research, the Personal Development Market, or what is often referred to as Self-Help, was estimated at $48.4 billion in 2024. That same market is expected to grow to $67 billion by 2030.

Industry legends like Napoleon Hill, Dr. Norman Vincent Peale, Tony Robbins, Wayne Dwyer, and Stephen R. Covey, along with a newer generation of authors, such as Jack Canfield, Rick Warren, and James Cleary, attempt to help people break through anxiety and depression, improve self-worth, and engage in personal growth. Tens of millions of books are sold each year and translated into languages across the globe. Millions attend live seminars, listen to podcasts, and sign up for online coaching.

Book titles read like maps to a better life: *Think and Grow Rich, 7 Habits of Highly Effective People, Unlimited Power, The Power of Positive Thinking, Atomic Habits, The Purpose-Driven Life, Chicken Soup for the Soul,* and more.

Meanwhile, the size of the psychology industry in the United States, composed of psychologists, social workers, and marriage counselors, was estimated at $36.6 billion in 2025. According to Becker's Behavioral Health, the US behavioral health market was valued at more than $89 billion in 2024 and is expected to reach $165 billion by 2034.[11]

It's not just a mental health crisis. It's a crisis of purpose. It's a crisis of alignment. It's a crisis of meaning. And we know it's likely to get worse.

I'm a huge fan of these authors and their work. I believe that anyone willing to take the initiative to improve their life and their mental health should be applauded. I believe so much in the power of the mind that, over time, I have read all of the books mentioned above and many more like them. But what I've never understood is why we wait until adulthood to think about the wiring of our brain?

The majority of this industry is targeted at adults and addresses mental states that are essentially broken or misaligned and in need of REPAIR. Why do we wait until it's broken? Why do we wait until adulthood to discover the skills and tools necessary for a vibrant, productive life and a healthy mind? Why aren't we building strong mental frameworks into our children from an early age, so these structures are hardwired in and more permanent? Instead of focusing the conversation on "Rewiring our brains", why don't we wire them correctly from the start?

NATURE VS. NURTURE

The jury is out. During the industrial era of education, an argument raged between the idea of natural intelligence—nature—and the effects of the environment a child grows up in—nurture. The first problem with this argument is that under the industrial model, nature only really measured the IQ portion of organic intelligence. It never had a way of accounting for creative intelligence, or that so many "smart" people never come up with truly revolutionary ideas. Second, years of research have shown that nurture has a tremendous impact on all parts of a human being, including their ability to perform on tests. In fact, nurture improves nature under the right conditions and damages nature under the wrong conditions.

We have the capability to increase and improve the brain's capacity to generate new ideas. We have the capacity to build divergent and alternative thoughts. We have the capacity to build a highly agile and adaptable brain. We can infuse self-confidence, healthy risk-taking, and resilience. The result isn't just a highly imaginative and creative child, it's a mentally healthy child that is ready to take on the challenges of an ever-changing and increasingly fast twenty-first century.

THE OPPORTUNITY

While anyone can use the information contained in this book to increase imagination and creativity at any age, there is no more important period in life when we create the composition of our permanent mental framework than in early childhood. During the critical stages of development between the ages of five and ten, the brain continues to undergo reorganization, fine-tuning, and remodeling of existing circuits and networks. Myelination continues in areas like the corpus callosum and subcortical areas, enhancing the speed and efficiency of communication between brain regions. Brain activity begins to specialize. At this age, children develop increased problem-solving skills, improved attention spans, and enhanced memory. Their vocabulary expands as they focus on reading, writing, and vocal expression. They learn social concepts such as morality, fairness, empathy, and compassion.

I'm a believer that we only get about ten years to truly influence the biological, psychological, neurological, and sociological foundations our children will carry into the future. Every parent with a teenager has had the experience of waking up one morning and realizing that the adorable little bunnies that used to follow us around the house full of giggles and curiosity, desperately in need of our approval and affections, have somehow been replaced by some grumpy, intolerant, narcissistic, and isolationist ogre who can barely stand the fact that we are breathing. We certainly don't have anything interesting or important to say. For any good parent, the moment is heartbreaking, albeit a natural and necessary part of healthy development if a child is ever going to stand on their own.

> **WE ONLY GET ABOUT TEN YEARS TO TRULY INFLUENCE THE BIOLOGICAL, PSYCHOLOGICAL, NEUROLOGICAL, AND SOCIOLOGICAL FOUNDATIONS OUR CHILDREN WILL CARRY INTO THE FUTURE.**

That means we get a total of about ten years, from somewhere around the age of two to the age of twelve, to have maximum impact and forge the permanent traits that will allow an emerging adult to maintain the joyful curiosity and exploration that innovation demands. While the human spirit wants to believe that anything is possible, the world around us can be a constant portent of negative messaging. From the time they begin to express their very first dream, children are faced with an incredible wall of doubters and naysayers waiting to tell them what is not possible and what they cannot do. Our goal is to develop an unassailable fortress of positive self-worth, endless curiosity and imagination, and empowered thinking.

The most critical opportunity for us to focus on our child's creativity and imagination is within these years, not only because we can develop the right brain patterns, but because we have the opportunity to preserve a great deal of the connections already given to us during the earliest stages of brain development. Through attention, we can determine the structure, importance, and strength of the connections we will need for imagination and creativity.

This is the time when we need to establish an environment where creativity thrives. As Rick Rubin describes it in *The Creative Act*:

> A space so free of normal overpacked conditions of our minds that it functions as a vacuum. Drawing down the ideas the universe is making available… This freedom is not as difficult to achieve as one might think. We all start with it. As children, we experience less interference between receiving ideas and internalizing them. We accept new information with delight instead of making comparisons to what we already believe; we live in the moment rather than worrying about future consequences; we are spontaneous more than analytical; we are curious, not jaded. Even the most ordinary experiences in life are met with a sense of awe.[12]

There is a time to be six years old. There is a time to be seven and a time to be eight. And NONE of these is the same as what it means to be thirteen or sixteen or twenty. Once a child reaches early adolescence, around the age of twelve, they will take on a whole new level of challenges. Puberty and hormones kick in. Social pressures rise to extreme levels as children navigate intense emotions while attempting to forge their identities. The world can be tricky, confusing, and, at times, cruel. They are often and repeatedly warned that they will soon be adults. As they hit high school and early adulthood, they spend most of their time preparing for jobs, careers, marriage, children, money, houses, car payments, and more. Stress stacks on top of stress and more stress. If we wait and react to what we see in the teenage years, patterns and behaviors that have been hardwired in are much more difficult to change.

We need to preserve childhood for as long as possible, and during that critical time, we need to build people who are capable of thriving. Not just through the difficult challenges of growing up, but also the unique challenges of an ever-changing and fast-paced world. The good news is we have the power to do just that.

Watch your thoughts, they become your words; watch your words, they become your actions; watch your actions, they become your habits; watch your habits, they become your character; watch your character, it becomes your destiny.

—Lao Tzu

So what are the goals for building powerful imaginations?

At the highest level, here is some of what we are trying to accomplish:

1. Creating a big, beautiful database in a child's mind. The more we learn, the more we see, the more we hear, taste, and smell. The more we explore, the more we experience, the deeper and broader the buckets we have from which to draw upon.
2. Creating incredible, robust, and fast networks of superhighways and bridges that connect as many parts of the mind as possible. Lowering the gates to some of the most challenging areas of the brain and hidden pathways.
3. Creating a mind that naturally seeks alternatives and enjoys the path less traveled.
4. Creating a system of access and control where the user understands its operations and has the power to influence its functions and outcomes.
5. Creating patterns and habits biased toward action, trial, and error, and the resilient pursuit of ideas.

We accomplish this in a variety of ways, but primarily through Intention, Environment, Skills, and Training.

INTENTION

If you are hoping that we can do nothing while the entire world goes through incredible disruption and change, and somehow, we'll all be okay, I wish you luck. I would point to the damage done with our apathy toward the impact of social media, despite our awareness and acknowledgement of what was happening.

Creating a generation that is imaginative, creative, adaptive, resilient, capable of deep focus, and able to navigate a world with an ever-changing set of rules and requirements can only be done through intention. We must position these skill sets and mental frameworks as a priority, and we must do it immediately. We cannot wait. The world is moving too fast.

ENVIRONMENT

Comedians and professors

I am going to take you on a quick journey with a discussion around two distinct paths. In their own way, each environment provides an example of how creativity is developed over time through our daily patterns and the world we inhabit.

Comedians

C'mon, admit it. We've all wondered what it would be like to stand in front of large crowds and make everyone laugh. Oh, to be loved by millions for bringing joy into their lives. We've all met someone who spends their entire day trying to be funny. The problem is, they're just not professionals. We all *want* to be funny, but most of us don't want to spend our lives trying to make it as a comedian. Everyone would love to make millions like Kevin Hart, Will Ferrell, or Adam Sandler. But few of us want to spend years of our lives away from home, living in dumpy hotels for low pay on the path to stardom.

Those who really want to be a comedian risk everything and obsess over what it means to be funny. First, they're observational. They spend their time observing the world. They work odd jobs to find time to think. And when they reach some baseline level of success, they head out on the road to test their ideas and refine their jokes. While most of us are at work, grinding away at whatever pays our salary, comedians are on the road, grinding away at being funny. They don't have a job to show up for at eight a.m., and their minds aren't filled with spreadsheets or project deadlines. They think, observe, and write all day, and test their ideas against the crowd at night. Then they do it again and again.

There is a reason they are funnier than you. They work really hard at it. Comedians focus on the process. They spend their days wandering around and looking for colorful insights that we have all missed. They have trained their brains to look for these absurdities all around us. The result of all this thinking, trying, and revising is a well-tuned mind built around comedy.

Why do we love comedians so much? They make us laugh, but way deeper than that is that their profound way of connecting us with our own humanity, our own folly, our own stupidity, in a way that is insightful and yet harmless at the same time. What is actually happening? Well, in most cases, comedians have the gift of connecting seemingly random events in their lives and connecting them to our own, often in a way that we have not put together. That's the very definition of creativity and imagination.

> **COMEDIANS MAKE US LAUGH AND CONNECT US WITH OUR HUMANITY, FOLLY, AND STUPIDITY.**

Most well-known comedians have spent many years perfecting their craft. Sometimes in front of the mirror alone, then perhaps in front of family and friends, then a long journey of small, unrecognized comedy clubs, basically getting in front of anyone who will listen to their jokes.

Throughout the process, they are testing and revising, learning what jokes make people laugh, learning a storytelling style that impacts the audience. Eventually, when they have mastered the art of the insight, the art of storytelling, the art of presentation and timing, and if they are "lucky" enough, they begin to take flight. They are called "hilarious", make their way into television and film, and at the highest level, fill stadiums. But none of this is by accident. Yes, these are people who are naturally funny, but few are "creative geniuses" without years of prioritizing funny and placing themselves in a position to exercise and grow their talents.

Professors

In many ways, we don't think of academics as being creative. They live within the safety of a protected cocoon; they often have stable incomes and don't risk their livelihoods in the way an entrepreneur might. A fair criticism for many in the academic world is that their ideas often fail to work in the complexity of the real world.

That being said, there is little doubt that, over the last one hundred years, brilliant ideas and the foundation of many advancements were either incubated or nurtured within these environments. How is that possible? In my opinion, academics have several advantages over the rest of us when it comes to pursuing ideas.

The academic environment offers the opportunity for pontification. Many academic schedules are filled with holes to allow for these pursuits. Like comedians, professors are not tasked with worrying about spreadsheets, sales numbers, or product launches like many of us with "regular" jobs. Idea generation and testing are often considered a daily part of the job. Most tenured professors are required to do three things:

- Publish research and papers to advance their field of study.

- Apply for grants, which bring money and resources to the universities and research teams.
- Bring recognition to the university, which will hopefully lead to increased enrollment and additional funding.

Because of their long histories of research, a large portion of available funds for exploration and development flows in their direction from private endowments, government grants, and partnerships with large corporations.

There's no doubt that the best institutions attract the brightest minds and can be incredibly fertile grounds for creativity and innovation. Many professors have launched successful technology companies out of research labs in places like Stanford and MIT. Dr. Robert Cade famously launched Gatorade out of the University of Florida after researching the effects of heat on football players. After Alexander Fleming discovered penicillin, a group of professors and researchers at the University of Oxford successfully took it from the lab to the clinic, saving millions from death by infection. But the same outcomes might likely be available to many more who:

- Had the time and opportunity to consider their ideas and nurture them towards reality.
- Had substantial access to all the most relevant information, the brightest minds, the best technology, and the latest advancements in the field.
- Had the resources to build teams, buy equipment and supplies necessary to test their theories and advance their knowledge, along with those around them.
- Had the ability to share these ideas and outcomes with the entire world without gatekeepers and naysayers blocking the road and killing ideas before their birth.

One reason we hold entrepreneurs in such high regard is that they often have to accomplish all of these things without any of the structures, time, and resources available to academics and without the security of a salary that pays their rent and feeds their families. In recent years, we've seen many of these idea factories move out of the academic environments to incubators like Silicon Valley's Y Combinator and legendary investor Peter Thiel's Thiel Fellowship.

The point here is that creativity and innovation are built in many ways. The common themes of time, energy, and focus necessary to create are fundamental in the framework.

PERSPIRATION AND PREPARATION (*SKILLS AND TRAINING*)

On June 28, 2025, Ilia Topuria, the Spanish-Georgian MMA featherweight champion, won the UFC Lightweight title, making him one of a handful of people to ever win the championship belt in two weight divisions. As of July 1, 2025, he was considered the pound-for-pound best fighter in the world for the Men's division. Quite an accomplishment.

In the post-fight interview, Topuria responded to a reporter's question by saying, "I just came to collect my belt. I already won it in the training session."

The words might seem to be the confident bravado of a person who has just conquered their domain in front of the world, but the concept that "the fight is won in the gym" is a well-worn expression known by just about anyone connected to the sports world. No less than "The Greatest", Muhammad Ali, is attributed with his own version: "The fight is won or lost far away from the witnesses – behind the lines, in the gym, and out there on the road, long before I dance under those lights."

Training for an MMA fight is a combination of traditional Boxing and Muay Thai, with a dose of American wrestling and Brazilian Jiu-Jitsu thrown in. The best can't be good in only one area; they have to be good in all areas.

What does "the fight is won in the gym" look like for a UFC fighter? These elite athletes have to acquire a long list of high-level skills and techniques along with world-class physical conditioning to compete as a professional:

- Long-distance running for developing endurance in the lungs and legs.
- Hours of jump rope for balance, coordination, and endurance.
- Thousands of hours on the heavy bag to build power.
- Thousands of hours on the speed bag for hand-eye coordination.
- Thousands of hours on the mats practicing wrestling and Jiu-Jitsu.
- Thousands of hours doing footwork drills for movement, speed, and coordination.
- Shadow boxing to create comfort in the ring, practice technique, and visualize the opponent.
- Thousands of punches at boxing mitts worn by a coach to understand combinations, learn both offense and defense, and physically develop proper technique.
- Thousands of repetitive drills designed to create patterns of recognition and fast reflexes: straight jabs, right cross, hooks, head shots, body shots, and head movement.
- Light sparring to feel what it's like to face an opponent and practice everything they have learned.
- Heavy sparring to see how well a fighter can withstand extreme pressure and test their limits.
- Weight training for strength and power.

Most of us will never be a UFC champ because we don't like getting hit in the face and have no desire to fight other people. But even the best fighters in the world will never be a world champion like Ilia Topuria without the right skills, dedication, and training.

ONE MORE METAPHOR BEFORE MOVING ON

Imagine an orchestra taking the stage and attempting to perform with little to no prior rehearsal. The conductor is late, and everyone has forgotten their sheet music, but the show must go on. Extremely talented musicians have filled the orchestra chairs, but most have never played this piece before, and someone has arranged the seating incorrectly. The instruments are out of tune because no one bothered to check. As the curtain opens, no one knows the timing of the piece, the exact notes, or where to start or join in.

What should have been a beautiful and majestic symphony capable of raising the spirit and invoking tears of joy turns into a cacophony of noise resembling a chorus of howling dogs, frightened geese, and hungry alley cats.

It shouldn't surprise anyone that creativity fails when we have developed few of the skills necessary to imagine, a poor understanding of how to operate the machinery, no time or energy to create, our focus drawn away and occupied by other matters, and absolutely zero preparation or rehearsal.

True creative geniuses are rare, and yes, some people are exceptionally gifted by nature, but there are far more successful and capable creatives who have built their success through years of focus, hard work, and building knowledge and skill.

Effort matters. Dedication matters. Time and energy matter. Focus matters.

Creative people are endlessly curious. Some are curious about everything, but more often, incredibly curious about the things that draw their attention. They are willing to take deep, deep dives, sometimes to the point of obsession. That curious nature leads them to pursue things to the nth degree, leading to what many of us call passion. While pursuing these passions, their minds are open. They are willing to try anything that might yield the result they are looking for. They are willing to fail, repeatedly. They grow tired. They grow exhausted, just like the rest of us, but they try again. They are willing to reset, sometimes throwing away everything they have tried before. They are willing to discard assumptions that yield no results. It's the willingness to take themselves down this road time and time again that we might call purpose.

The result of all of this work is what many people perceive to be *imagination*. The wellspring of ideas comes from a genuine curiosity that has been honed through time and effort to produce alternative starting points and seek connections, a brain willing and able to comply with creative demands through years of building *capacity*.

This chapter is about building capacity. A factory designed to generate ideas.

The typical approach to Imagination.

Figure 3.1

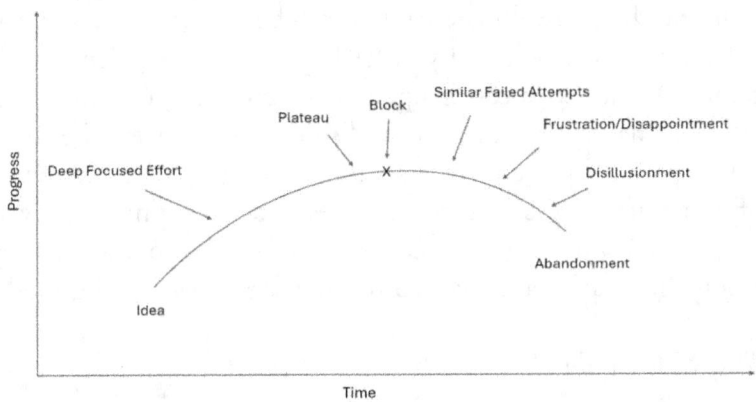

Why do so many of us struggle to come up with new or original ideas? As we have been discussing, most of us haven't built the framework and tools for active imagination. So when we attempt to use our imagination, our effort usually resembles Figure 3.1 above.

Often, we have an idea, whether prompted by work or our own desires for something new or original. It can be an invention, a new business, or simply a way to solve a problem. Many times, there is some initial spark. But even if we are starting from scratch, we generally engage with purpose, enthusiasm, energy, and effort. We are willing to work on it until our batteries run out. Somewhere along the path, the effort plateaus, and we reach a point where the energy is gone, and all forward motion has come to a halt. In the writer's world, everyone loves to refer to this as writer's block. For all of us, it's the same. The ideas we need simply aren't coming.

We continue working to the best of our abilities, usually in a loop of similar failed attempts, until we end up in a world of frustration. Enough attempts, enough failures, and we reach a sufficient level of disappointment. Disillusioned with our ability to break through the impasse, we give up and eventually abandon the cause altogether. This can be a quick loop; an idea flashes in your head, and you let it go almost as quickly as it came. Or the loops can happen at the end of a long journey, after you have put your heart and soul into a concerted effort. Either way, the pattern is the same. When this pattern happens often enough, we convince ourselves that we are not creative, and the act of giving up becomes a habit. This follows us our whole life if our brain received this message in early childhood.

The Wylde Loop

Figure 3.2

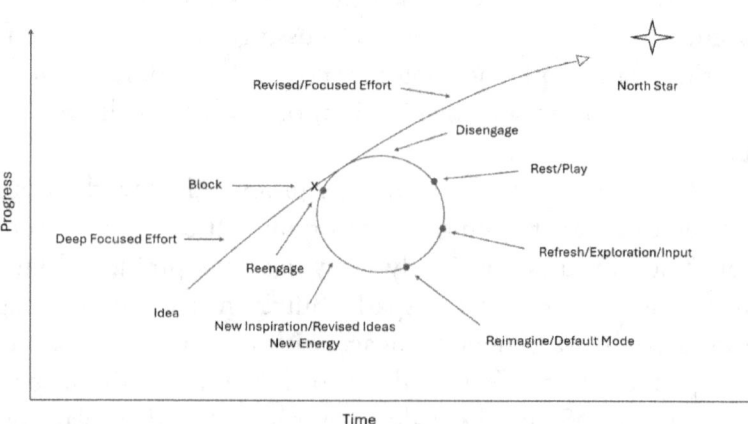

The Wylde Loop shows us a different approach to the same problem. It starts in the same manner. We have an itch we need to scratch. We jump in with two feet and go to work. If we are serious, we put in time and energy until we hit a block. But rather than giving up, we go on a *walkabout*.

THE WALKABOUT

When people get stuck while pursuing an idea, we refer to it as a block. In some form or another, that's exactly what it is. The conscious mind is tired and has basically stopped functioning, and the subconscious has lost its way or hit a wall. If we are in flow, we can often lose sight of exactly where we are, or we are so committed to the act that we begin to sabotage our own efforts. The most common form is what I like to call digging straight down. We continue the same pursuit, in the same way, over and over again, without much variance. In essence, because our brains are tired, we have stopped generating alternatives. We are repeating the same pattern, hoping for a different outcome. The entire art of imagination is the ability to create and consider options or variances. So how do we help the brain come up with a different way of looking at the same problem? I call it the Walkabout.

Your brain needs a break. It's that simple. We all know what this feels like. It's likely the number one driver of our addiction to cell phones. I don't believe anyone wants to lose hours every day staring at a 3x5 electronic device. Ask them. Ask yourself if that's what you dreamed of doing when you reached adulthood. We just needed to step away for a second, and the next thing we knew, it was time to go to bed.

The term walkabout is very often associated with the Aboriginal people of Australia and thought of as a journey through the wilderness. The goal is to get away, or go elsewhere, and roam and explore until the mind is satisfied and it's time to return home. History and culture are filled with versions of this act—Moses and the mountain, Jesus and the desert—where the journey often holds spiritual significance. In other ways, the journey is a trip away from the conscious into the subconscious, and the return brings a new form of knowledge.

For our purposes, we can think of it this way: we are stuck and need a fresh look at our problem, so we take a break. Rather than stare into our cell phones, we are going to take a break with *intention*. No need to spend forty days and forty nights away. Our walkabouts can be for an hour, a day, or a week, and our walkabouts should be fun.

The four Rs of the Walkabout:

1. Rest.

    This R is meant to be exactly what it sounds like. We want to rest our brain from all the *thinking*. We want to reduce stress, enjoy the moment, put a smile on our face, and maybe laugh a little. Read a book for pleasure, see a movie, take a walk, or watch some television. Take some time with friends. Eat a wonderful dinner. Play, play, and play some more. Do anything but think. I would only suggest avoiding one thing: the endless death scroll of the cell phone. I will dive into why later.

2. Refresh.

    Hopefully, a Rest period will end with you feeling refreshed in some way. So why have we listed this separately? The first R is more about resting physically and restoring our batteries for another go. This R is about resetting our brain, giving it more ammunition, and helping it find new pathways. The main goals of this period are to explore and add information to our wonderful database. In this phase, we can read and view more books and videos on the same subject with intention, seeking a different approach. We can listen to lectures on our field or by people we respect in our industry. Or we can maintain our distance and add experience and knowledge distinct from our current pursuit. Take in art. Spend time in nature. Learn a totally new skill. I like to call this the input phase. We welcome any and all *input*. We want to *expand* our mental framework. More information. More experience. When we are talking about children, this time needs to be as fun as possible. The more fun the experience, the more information their wonderful brains absorb.

3. Reimagine.

The walkabout is a powerful tool for moving between the conscious and the subconscious, as discussed in the previous chapter. During the active pursuit of an idea, we generally focus all our conscious effort on solving a problem. The first two Rs have been the process of moving away from the conscious and *toward* the subconscious. During the third R, we are at our farthest point away from the active and moving toward default mode. The idea here is to generate new ideas and starting points before returning to the active pursuit. This is when we want our mind to be deepest in the forest. The goal is free association. If we have rested our mind sufficiently, it has energy for the task. If we have refreshed our mind significantly, new sparks are firing, and new seeds are flowing. Now we just have to let them *connect*.

The art of this phase is to help our mind go silent, wander, and explore its own universe. We want to actively teach our children how to daydream. None of this will ever work by telling a five- or six-year-old, "You need to daydream." We need to develop this skill through experience. There must be "quiet time." In kindergarten, we used to take naps. Hopefully, some still do. But we need to train people in the art of "quiet time" up and through adulthood. We can help build daydreaming using simple prompts. I will talk about many in the next two chapters, but one example is the "blank page" exercise, where all we instruct them to do is "draw anything" and then leave them alone for thirty minutes. No expectations. No goals. We simply want their minds to wander.

> **WE WANT TO ACTIVELY TEACH OUR CHILDREN HOW TO DAYDREAM.**

4. Reengage.

This is the proverbial return home. Having discovered new ideas, we are ready to give it another try. We resurface from the subconscious refreshed and ready to engage. Our satchel is full of new thoughts and concepts, and more importantly, we are once again *inspired*. We aggressively head back into the conscious space and return to active pursuit of our ideas and/or mission.

As you can see, the Wylde Loop is an intentional effort to create maximum opportunity for imagination by cycling between the conscious and subconscious. Learning to operate within the loop becomes a *pattern* that our brain begins to recognize. It begins to emulate this process on its own until one day it becomes automatic. When in need, your brain naturally knows what to do to come up with fresh and innovative ideas. Then we'll need to turn *patterns* into *habits*. But before we move to the next level, you may have noticed something I haven't mentioned in the Wylde Loop—the *North Star*.

NORTH STAR

The North Star is not the same as a goal. It's a guided path. It lets us know what direction we are headed in and whether we are heading in the right direction. It can be seen no matter where we are in the journey. It can help us when we are lost in the wilderness to find our way home. It cannot be moved or concealed. It stands at the front of our mind like a beacon in the night, unwavering and always present.

We absolutely want to teach children goal setting, breaking down goals, and accomplishing things one step at a time. These should be taught and ingrained from an early age, so that when children look at a problem, nothing is insurmountable. But the North Star is a bit more powerful. In the mind, it sits above goals. At its grandest scale, we can interpret this as having purpose. On the smaller end, we can associate it with *meaning*. Meaning gives us a *connection* to the pursuit. Connection stands at the very heart of *intrinsic motivation*. When people are personally connected to an idea, a mission, or a goal, they won't give up that pursuit so easily. The greater the meaning, the stronger the connection. They are much more inclined to suffer failures, weather disappointment, and try again. This is extremely important when reaching our imagination. If there are no markers, there are no rules and no precedent, the most powerful force keeping us moving forward is the desire itself. If we can develop a North Star framework into our children's mental habits, they will be capable of anything. Now let's talk about how we turn these patterns into habits.

The Wylde Method

Figure 3.3

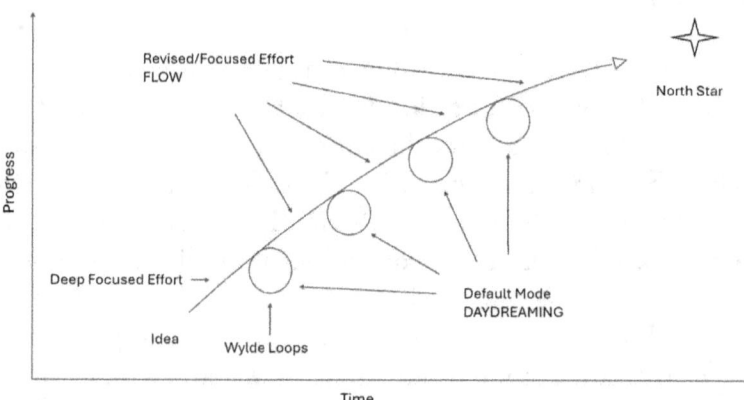

Secret #4: The highest levels of creativity are established by repeatedly moving between patterns of free association in Default Mode and the deep focus of Flow.

Ok, there you have it, Secret #4 of imagination. For lack of a better term to describe the process, I am using the "Wylde Method." I took that from the Montessori Method and the Pomodoro Technique, both of which I admire greatly. A bit presumptuous, I know, but you can call it whatever you like.

If the secret to creating a vivid imagination is our capacity to move between the conscious and the subconscious (the Wylde Loop), then the secret to being *creative* is the ability to move between states of deep focus and deep states of free association. A *bridge* between *default mode* and *flow*. We have both *access* and *control* of our most focused mind and our most explorative mind.

The idea of the Wylde Method is to constantly create experiences that move our children through these patterns on a daily basis. Its mechanics follow the path of the Wylde Loop time and again. Prompt ideas, create North Stars, challenge them to pursue those ideas, teach them how to rest their mind, allow them to play, expand their world and experiences, create fun and exciting games that hone their skills, practice, practice, practice, give them time to ponder, pontificate and wander the universe in their mind, encourage it, prioritize it, and then repeat as often as you can.

The Wylde Method is *designed* to:

- Continuously build new pathways in the mind.
- Strengthen existing pathways and increase their speed and efficiency.
- Continually expand their world and their base of knowledge.
- Develop patterns into skills, skills into habits.
- Open up the bridge between the conscious and the subconscious.
- Oscillate between modes of Deep Focus and Daydreaming.
- Create Access and Control of these mental frameworks.

By mastering the Wylde Loop, we gain the tool sets of accessing our imaginations on demand. Once we've mastered the Wylde Method, we can call on imagination to assist us in any pursuit or any endeavor. We create patterns in our mind that develop the habits of creativity. By practicing these habits repeatedly, we reach a state where we essentially *are* creative. Creators don't just create, creators are.

WHAT THIS LOOKS LIKE IN REAL LIFE

Life is not perfect; it's messy. If you thought you were going to pick up this book and magically transform yourself or your child overnight into an imagination powerhouse, you are likely mistaken. Like life, the road can be hard. It takes work and commitment.

I'll refer back to my morning routine for a second. I would be lying to you if I told you this works like clockwork, every day, without fail. There are many mornings when I fall back asleep on the couch. Could have had a long day previously, trouble sleeping, or a lack of enthusiasm for the new day. For whatever reason, I just don't have it in me. Sometimes I'll blow that whole morning trying to catch a few more *zzzzs*. Sometimes I will do anything BUT sit down and write: dishes, laundry, shower, shave, pay bills, or pay taxes. And yes, yes, yes, oh lord, how I hate to admit this, YES! Sometimes I pick up that darn phone! I am as guilty as anyone of losing three hours of my life in absolute nonsense before raising my head to see the sun.

But here is the thing. My habits are so ingrained that they won't allow this to continue very long. For every seven days of the week, I pretty much perform my morning routine at least five of those days. That's a minimum of fifteen hours per week, intensely floating between my conscious and subconscious before I engage the world. That does not include daydreaming or falling asleep at night. That puts me way ahead of the competition.

By following the Wylde Method, we are not trying to develop solutions; we are developing *habits*. A person who knows how to do this can repeatedly daydream their way towards mind-wandering and free associations to repeatedly come up with new ideas, and can *apply* those ideas into focused attempts to materialize them into existence.

Here's an example of what these habits look like when pushed up against the challenges of the real world:

Figure 3.4

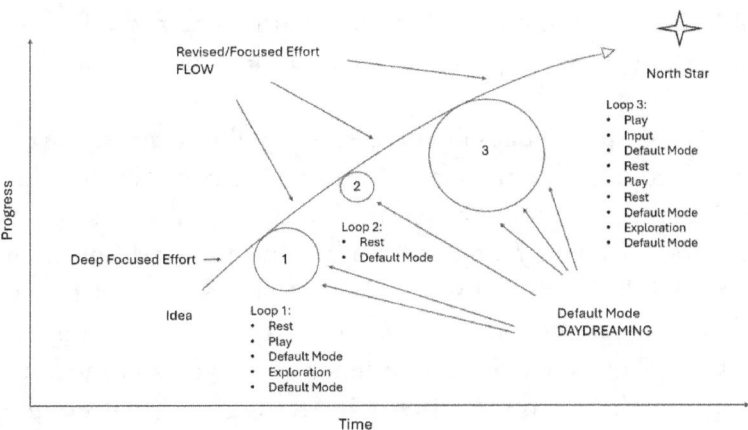

Figure 3.4 is a much more accurate representation of attempting to create Wylde Loops and follow the Wylde Method. We start with an idea and create some form of North Star for ourselves. It can be the pursuit of a single idea or a grand master plan. In the process of coming up with new ideas, we run into the typical roadblock. So, we move into a Wylde Loop with the intention of getting unstuck. In our first round, we

take some time off, we play a bit, we ponder a bit. Still doesn't feel right, so we go back into exploration. We try to find some new inspiration or knowledge to move us forward. That exploration sparks a thought and sends us back into default mode to work it out. When we believe we have something to work with, we head back into the active phase and hopefully reach a state of flow. Then we hit another roadblock.

This time around, we step away for a minute to think. After a moment of rest, our mind drifts back into some free associations, and "ah-ha!" we come up with an idea. This time, we are absolutely sure we have the answer. We work feverishly from this new angle at lightning speed until suddenly, and to our great surprise, we hit another roadblock, a dead end. Because we are so well-trained, our natural habits kick in, and rather than accept defeat, we eventually head back into a Wylde Loop.

This time, it doesn't come so naturally. Because we are pretty fed up, we immediately head out to play. We just need to NOT think about this at all. We play until we can't play anymore. We take a detour for a bit into the world of input. Most of it has nothing to do with the North Star, but occasionally we are tempted to read up a bit and learn more about our mission. The new information sends us into default mode for a bit. We drift into some pretty interesting stuff, but nothing worth talking about. We're still tired, so we look for more rest. Pure enjoyment. Free laughs. Time with family. We play for a bit and decide we're not done resting.

Eventually, the rest ends up in some much-needed *time alone*, and our brain begins to wander. Quite accidentally, we find ourselves in default mode. We get the seeds of an idea, but it's not fully formed, so we rush back out to explore. Only this time, we are exploring with full intention. We are actively searching for information that will add to or solidify this delicate germ of an idea. When we feel as though we have gathered enough kernels, we hurry back into a dark cave and try to put all of the pieces together. Finally, we emerge with the "right idea" and take it all the way home to our North Star.

This is how the loops actually work. The above process could take a week, a month, or even years. For most of us, we would be trying to hit the North Star while working extra shifts, taking our kids to school, arguing with the phone company about our cell phone bill, dealing with a sick dog, and somehow trying to stay healthy. That is why habits are so important.

> **REAL LIFE MAKES YOU WANT TO CHECK YOUR SOCIAL MEDIA ACCOUNTS.**

THE BIGGEST SUPERPOWER

Superman has many powers:

1. Strength
2. Speed
3. Invincibility
4. Flight
5. Heat vision
6. X-ray Vision
7. Super hearing
8. And weirdest of all, super breath.

Together they make up the set of skills that make him sooo, well, *super*. The patterns and habits wrapped up in the Wylde Method make up a tool bag of incredible skills and capabilities that, combined, create an unassailable imagination. Every skill and trait is important to the development of our children. However, one stands above the rest when confronted with the pressure, resistance, and difficult nature of the real world.

One of the superpowers of the Wylde Method is the ability to go back after it, time and again, attacking problems from a different angle. It's a combination of resilience and imagination. Try A, and if A doesn't work, try B, and if B doesn't work, try C. How many of us would quit at B? How many people do you know who would continue all the way to Z? What about you? How resilient are you, and how many different angles do you think you would be able to come up with without burning out and eventually giving up?

Deeply embedded in the continual process of loops are the seeds of resilience. If a child has spent much of their early years trying and succeeding, they develop confidence. If part of their daily learning curve is to fail, they learn to associate failure with process, not identity. If they watch as their peers try and fail, then try and succeed, they assimilate the experience as a natural part of life. Bit by bit, they learn not to attach emotion to single points of failure. They use their mind to work themselves out of tight spots and adjust their paths. The access to their imagination allows them to see multiple options and various possibilities. Trying again requires the knowledge that there is another way, and the belief that this path might lead to success. Children well-rehearsed in attempting ideas aren't afraid to try, fail, and try again because they have learned the *art* of trying. In its highest form, we have done exceptionally well if we can teach them the *joy* of trying.

> **CHILDREN WELL-REHEARSED IN ATTEMPTING IDEAS AREN'T AFRAID TO TRY, FAIL, AND TRY AGAIN.**

Developing these habits at an early age and then hardwiring them into a child's permanent mental framework can make all the difference in the world.

THE LITTLE CONDUCTOR

Before leaving the chapter on imagination, I want to introduce you to the idea of *The Little Conductor*. Suppose your mind is an orchestra. It has multiple sections and a variety of instruments: strings, woodwinds, brass, and percussion. Occasionally, there's a piano or a vocalist. All the various parts make up a greater whole, with each contributing to the sound and texture.

Standing in the middle, the conductor has access to all this immense power to create sound. He wields that power with knowledge, confidence, passion, and creativity to deliver something special to the world.

The Little Conductor has access to and control over all facets of the mind and imagination. He easily commands broad functions like memory, attention, sight, sound, touch, feel, emotion, critical thinking, and higher reasoning. His skills include speed, agility, adaptability, resilience, and curiosity. He is a master of imagination and creativity.

He knows the sounds of every instrument and every possible combination in the mind. He can conduct solos, quartets, quintets, sonatas, concertos, or symphonies. He can perform across genres such as ballet and opera. He can transform a performance from classical to jazz, rock, or blues. Greatest of all, he can improvise.

The Little Conductor knows every road, river, and highway in his mind. He knows where all secrets are buried in dark forests and castle keeps. He has access to all parts of the brain and knows how to lower bridges and open gates. He can spend hours, days, or weeks traveling the subconscious and emerge with powerful ideas.

He takes in signals from the external environment and adjusts his thoughts and actions to meet the environment's demands. He knows how to successfully form relationships and connections with others and can successfully navigate the external world as well as his own internal one.

This is what we mean by *access* and *control*. This is where we reach the full potential of Creative Intelligence. My biggest hope in writing this book is that we will spend an extraordinary amount of time focused on building the skill sets of imagination and creativity in the earliest stages of childhood development. It is our responsibility to develop a little conductor in the mind of every child. Future generations depend on it.

Let's dive deep into how that is done.

Chapter 6

TRAINING THE LITTLE CONDUCTOR

WYLDE SCOTT

IT'S TIME TO TAKE CHILDHOOD BACK.

This is the worst-kept secret on the planet: *the System is Broken.* Over the past few centuries, we have seen incredible changes in the development of children based on the needs of the times or the transformations occurring throughout the world. We have emerged from a time when literacy and education were the luxury of only a privileged few. For most of history, life was based on some form of agriculture. Families were rewarded for having large numbers of kids, and their most valuable skill was to work the land. During the industrial revolution, families were thrown into cities, and children often worked solo or alongside their parents in factories. There was little need for true education beyond physical strength to clean or operate some form of machine, but by the end of the nineteenth century, the rapidly expanding needs of production led more children into schools. By the late twentieth century, the general pursuit of *more* education began to take hold as the *ideal* goal of university education became paramount. This was deemed absolutely necessary to participate in the newly formed *knowledge economy*. As we head into this new AI world and what might be described as a *post-knowledge era*, no one is quite sure what education should look like. Only one thing is certain: *Everyone* agrees the current system will not work.

EDUCATION IS AT WAR WITH ITSELF

Over the past ten years, we have witnessed the outbreak of war. I'm not speaking of the Ukraine, the Middle East, or any one of a thousand geopolitical skirmishes. I'm speaking of the war within the classroom.

Teachers are at war with parents. Parents are at war with school boards. Unions are at war with governments. Public Schools versus Charter Schools versus Private Schools versus Homeschooling. Technology-driven curricula versus *No Tech in Schools*. It goes on and on and on. The anger and disrespect of everyone's individual roles and possible contributions have become visceral. It reminds me of my favorite analogy, "the storm at sea."

> We're all on a ship together. The ship is lost at sea in a violent storm and is sinking. The captain, the first mate, and an admiral each shout conflicting commands to the crew on deck, who are confused or have stopped listening. While some passengers steal the silver, others tear the sails and chop at the masts to build fires and stay warm. A member of the aristocracy interrupts the captain to complain about last night's dinner. As one group of sailors plugs holes in the hull, another group removes them because there are not enough to go around. The remaining sailors below have given up and broken into barrels of rum. The one intelligent person aboard has quietly lowered the only lifeboat and paddled away from the ship's stern. If the goal is to sail the ship to safety, none of us is going to make it.

My question for all of us is this: *What about the children?*

Rather than argue out all of the varied grievances, I'd rather focus on that one-hundred-foot wave about to swallow us all. Let's start by talking about the system as a whole.

THE PROBLEM WITH EDUCATION

> **Secret # 5:** The modern educational system was not designed for your child.

Spend ten minutes reading up on where the biggest cracks are, and you'll quickly come to a discussion about the *industrial model*. As described at the start of this chapter, the base for the current model of mass education was designed more than one hundred years ago at the dawn of the industrial revolution. The original system was designed to establish basic literacy and skills that would facilitate the operation of large factories popping up in all industrialized nations. In the early stages, mandatory education wasn't fully enforced until after the 1920s. As more families moved into cities for work, more children flooded the schools. Still, most children exited the school system somewhere between twelve and fourteen to enter the workforce.

The structure of schools mimicked production lines. Children sat in neat rows while a teacher stood at the front and instructed. The model was entirely based on rules and conformity. Every child was taught the same material in exactly the same way. The output was intentionally designed to be a consistent product—a young adult capable of adding to the workforce. The end goal was production capacity, not healthy, imaginative children.

This model would set the tone for public education for the next one hundred years. Somewhere around the late 1970s and early 1980s, two things converged that would place nearly all the emphasis on encouraging children to attend university.

1. The offshoring of manufacturing to cheaper countries, such as China and the Far East, has led to the decimation of traditional manufacturing and the well-paying jobs in most of the West.
2. The dawn of the modern technology era set the need for a new type of worker—the college-educated, knowledge-based employee.

Rather than develop a new system of education, the industrial model was simply adapted to fit this new worker. The need for accountants, engineers, computer programmers, and office workers has replaced the traditional trades. The production machine remains largely in place today, churning out a different product.

Society has, in general, benefited from this model. Standards of living in Western industrial nations have risen considerably over the last century. More children are safe, housed, fed, and educated than at any period in history, which is why the system has endured so long without significant change. Companies have come to rely on the machine for the workforce they need. Governments have come to rely on a consistent employment and tax base for national stability and public harmony. There was little incentive for the system to transform.

As the twentieth century progressed into its final decades, cracks began to appear in the veneer. Unlike the general rise of all tides in the 1950s and 1960s, when America became the world's manufacturing leader, the technology revolution introduced some uncomfortable disruption. With the offshoring replacing many traditional jobs, the gains and benefits of a new economy were not shared by all. The gap between the haves and have-nots began to widen. Impacted most of all were inner-city neighborhoods and rural areas where factories had disappeared, and resources were low. Literacy rates, test scores, high school graduation rates, college attendance, and job prospects all began to decline dramatically in these areas as the century drew to a close.

> **ENACTED WITH THE BEST OF INTENTIONS, THE RESULT OF NCLB IS A WORSE SYSTEM THAN WE STARTED WITH.**

To address this rising disconnect, the United States government enacted the No Child Left Behind Act in 2002. NCLB, as it is most commonly known, aimed to improve education by increasing accountability for schools and providing more options for parents. The key aspects of the law were:

- Mandated annual testing in reading and math.
- Schools were held accountable for student performance, and those failing to meet Adequate Yearly Progress (AYP) faced consequences like public labeling, required improvement plans, and potential restructuring.
- Providing parents with options such as transferring their children to better-performing schools or receiving free tutoring services.
- Requiring teachers to be highly qualified in the subjects they teach.
- Using data from standardized tests to drive instruction, curriculum development, and school management.

While proponents highlighted improved test scores and increased options for parents, critics argued that it led to teaching to the test and narrowed the curriculum. The critics were right.

Enacted with the best of intentions, the result is a worse system than we started with. Curricula now take their orders from the top. The government set the standards, state boards and county school districts created plans for compliance, school administrators set the curriculum in their schools based on guidance from the school boards, and teachers followed suit within the classroom. Fearing financial repercussions, the government focused on the outcomes of testing. Educators responded by narrowing the curriculum and putting enormous pressure on test preparation. A new model emerged: Test-Prep-Test, where the entirety of a child's day became centered around sitting at a desk and preparing for the next test. Arts programs began to disappear, as did time to play. They removed any activity not perceived to improve performance on national testing standards from the classroom. Cheating scandals broke out as some teachers found ways to inflate the students' scores out of fear of losing their jobs.

Concerned people began to speak out about the impact of the industrial model as a whole and the new aggressive form of testing on the mental and physical health of children. Finally, they were willing to step up and ask

What about the children?

The most-watched TED Talk in the history of YouTube is a 2006 Montreal speech titled "Do Schools Kill Creativity?"[13] Sir Ken Robinson, a PhD in drama and theater education, was an internationally recognized leader in the development of creativity, innovation, and human potential. He advised governments, corporations, education systems, and some of the world's leading cultural organizations. He based his talk on his years in and around educational systems and an extension of his earlier book, *Out of Our Minds*. Robinson wasn't the first to challenge the traditional educational system, but he was certainly the most eloquent in arguing that it often stifled creativity rather than fostering it. His speech emphasized the importance of creativity in education, suggesting it is as vital as literacy. For years, he advocated new approaches to education, culminating in his groundbreaking book, *Creative Schools*, published in 2015.

Having myself been a huge advocate for the importance of imagination, I was a big fan. I have read most of his books and watched the TED Talk no less than twenty times. As he has for many people, Robinson has greatly influenced my thinking about how we might rewrite the solution. He was one of the first to describe the current path of education in linear terms:

> "College begins in kindergarten. The whole elementary and high school experience is designed to be a protracted system of university experience."
>
> "Our educational systems don't enable students to develop their natural creative powers. Instead, schools promote uniformity and standardization."[14]
>
> "They are damaging the prospects of countless young people… Many talented, brilliant people think they're not because the thing they were good at in school wasn't valued or was highly stigmatized."[15]
>
> "The revolution I am advocating for… is based on the value of the individual, the right to self-determination, our potential to evolve and live a fulfilled life, and the importance of civic responsibility."[16]

The overreliance on high-stakes testing undermines education and comes at the cost of creativity, critical thinking, and mental health. The outcomes have been devastating. Children are disinterested, disaffected, and disengaged. As stated previously, rates of anxiety, depression, and suicide have skyrocketed. Overdependence on medication is rampant. No human being is ever meant to spend eight hours chained to a desk, much less a happy, vibrant, energetic child.

Teachers are not immune to the effects of modern education either. Often disillusioned, disenfranchised, and tired, many are packing up and leaving the profession entirely. This happens faster and faster, with some burning out within a few years of beginning their career.

Many have stood up in the last twenty years to join the battle cry, but little has moved in most public institutions. The reason it hasn't worked is because we are trying to put a square peg into a round hole. As with the transition to a knowledge-based economy, we are aspiring to adapt creativity and imagination into a model built for standardization, conformity, and testing. It doesn't work.

THE LACK OF IMAGINATION

Before kids graduate from high school, they will spend more than fourteen thousand hours in the classroom. How much time are kids spending on developing their imaginations? I challenge you to find any research that shows education spends time on building imagination. You won't, I've tried. You'll find thousands of hours of research and curriculum dedicated to Science, Technology, Engineering, and Math (STEM), and far, far less time dedicated to specific instruction meant to build dreamers. Since high-stakes testing took over, no one has the time.

In most cases, students only have two opportunities to develop themselves outside of academic pursuits. One is in arts programs (If you can find one). In many schools across the US, for example, artists often develop as a merry band of misfits. With the extreme focus on academics, this group is generally identified sometime in middle school, and by high school, it becomes a small percentage of the general population. With the low importance placed on creative pursuits, such as music, art, and drama, these are often the first programs to be cut.

> **EVERYONE KNOWS THAT THE FIRST PROGRAMS TO GET CUT UNDER THE PRESSURE OF SCORES AND FUNDING ARE THE ARTS AND HUMANITIES.**

The tragedy of this form of thinking is that very often, the arts program is the only place where creativity is discussed or encouraged. Drama students undergo a tremendous amount of training in improv and alternative thinking. Creative writing students spend time training on how to develop characters, how to develop plots, and how to come up with ideas for new stories. Artists are encouraged to explore painting styles and palettes to find their voice as artists. While everyone else is busy *conforming*, this group is *exploring*. *Everyone* knows that the first programs to get cut under the pressure of scores and funding are the arts and humanities.

The other group I will mention is student-athletes. An important part of the twenty-first-century mindset will be the ability to work through challenges. The most valuable activity in this regard for developing these skills in children has traditionally been sports. Sports are filled with excellent motivations and positive psychology. Young athletes are taught habits and mental frameworks around the need for hard work to succeed, the resilience of not giving up, the spirit of a good fight, and fair play. Coaches invest considerable time attempting to layer strong mental toughness over their athletes' physical talents and training.

Both of these are brilliant avenues for gaining some of the skills needed to thrive in the future, but few artists become athletes, and few athletes will become artists. Creativity rarely creeps over into the athletic world, as their focus is narrowed to fit the needs of the sport. Drills in football are different than soccer, and most are designed with the *rules of the game* in mind. Most artists are never trained in mental toughness. In fact, artists are usually among the more sensitive personalities amongst us and often struggle with finding the balance between personality and social interaction.

The sadder fact is that most students will never be a known artist or a star athlete. The majority of students will have neither the repeated experience of creative exploration nor the intense resilience of an athlete formed through years of training. None of these programs understands how to focus on these traits holistically, and few children, if any, start the deep training and exploration prior to the age of ten.

If, from the time small children can read, we begin to remove the influence of creativity and imagination and replace it with memorization and conformity, is it any wonder that a tiny percentage of adults hold what we would consider to be a high range of creative capacity?

THE UNIVERSITY SYSTEM

Here's another big pronouncement: Just as the very idea of a *job* will die with the twenty-first century, so will the university system as we know it. In many ways, they only have themselves to blame.

With the switch to a knowledge-based economy in the 1980s, an explosion of white-collar jobs came online to fill the needs of the market. The educational system responded by essentially placing the university smack in the middle of the path between the child and future employment, while also decrying traditional jobs that did not require a college degree in the process.

The only thing that became important from the time a child entered kindergarten was performing academically so that they could out-compete the millions of other children trying to get into college. Washed away were the foundations of a healthy childhood. The university system found itself in the catbird seat, becoming the most powerful entity in the chain of upward mobility. Its reaction could be described as an abuse of power.

If you traveled throughout the US and toured modern campuses today, you would find institutions that prioritize a business model over the actual education of their students. Rather than rigorous academic training and preparation for the real world, undergraduate studies feel more like a four-year vacation at a luxury resort. Campuses have been redesigned to attract high school students like bees to honey:

- Apartments whose amenities rival the best buildings in Manhattan.
- Vast food choices across campus, replacing the old, limited cafeterias.

- World-class gyms and fitness facilities for students, faculty, and staff.
- Pools, parks, and leisure sports ensure no student ever becomes bored.

Practically anyone with a mediocre GPA immediately had access to a comfortable, practically affluent lifestyle—no need to wait for the old-fashioned values of hard work and a successful career. *Everyone* signed up because *no one had to pay for it*. Banks colluded with universities to create a false financial system where virtually everyone was guaranteed a loan without considering the ability to repay it or weighing the potential value of the investment. Governments supported the plan as statistics regarding higher education continued to trend in the right direction. Parents joined the fray because they were told they *had to* if they wanted their kids to have a prosperous life. What parent would say no?

As Sir Ken Robinson astutely concluded: Education has become "one of the world's biggest businesses."[17]

Over the long run, sticker prices at four-year colleges grew much faster than prices in the broader economy and faster than real wages. The Georgetown University Center on Education and the Workforce found that earnings for young workers with a bachelor's degree increased by only 19 percent over the past four decades, while college costs rose by 169 percent.[18] Families responded by incurring massive amounts of debt.

How did Universities respond to the crises of borrowing? By telling students they needed *more* education. As students entered the workforce and found they could not find jobs or salaries high enough to maintain their accustomed lifestyle, they ran back to the security and safety of the university system, postponing their entry into the workforce. *The Hechinger Report*, based on research conducted at the University of

Tennessee, found that universities and colleges vastly expanded their graduate offerings to accommodate students, listing more than three times as many by 2021 as they had in 2005.[19] Universities were happy to assist students who increased their borrowing.

Borrowing for graduate school accounts for a significant portion of the rise in student debt. For example, borrowing for graduate school accounted for about half of the outstanding student debt as of 2017. Students kept borrowing and borrowing and borrowing to keep up with the ever-rising cost of education. Over the last twenty years, total student debt has risen by over 260 percent from approximately $500 billion to a staggering $1.8 trillion in 2025.[20] Student loan debt is now the second-highest consumer debt category after mortgages. For shame!

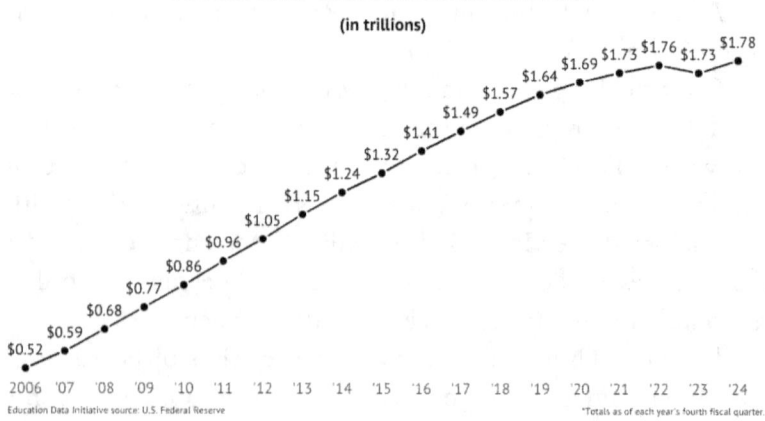

Chart Courtesy of Hanson, Melanie. "Student Loan Debt Statistics," EducationData.org, August 8, 2025, https://educationdata.org/student-loan-debt-statistics.

BLOAT AND BUREAUCRACY

The Party seeks power entirely for its own sake. We are not interested in the good of others; we are interested solely in power.

—George Orwell, *1984*

We normally associate corruption with the abuse of power in exchange for *money*. There is a far more common type of corruption associated with the misalignment of responsibility and *purpose*. It most often occurs in large institutions where the leadership has forgotten what the entity's original mission is and instead focuses on the survival and power of the entity. We can see this in governments all over the world, where the politicians have forgotten the people. It also happens in business when companies overlook the needs of their customers. It occurs in nearly every massive bureaucracy. The entity itself and the people who make their living off the entity become paramount, and the end user or beneficiary is irrelevant. A special form of corruption occurs when the money being spent is disconnected from the individual or persons for whom the benefit is intended. The decision-makers are insulated from any responsibility or accountability. The result is usually disastrous for everyone involved.

Because the money borrowed for higher education did not immediately affect the buyer or the producer (because the repayment was pushed years down the road), both the cost of producing higher education and the value of the end product have been largely corrupted.

In researching the rising costs of higher education, I came across an article that highlights the impact of this misalignment. In February 2024, *The Bowdon Review* published "Death By a Thousand Emails: How Administrative Bloat is

Killing American Higher Education." I want to share some of the author Lance Dininio's insights below:

- For its fewer than five thousand undergraduate students, Yale proudly employs an army of over 5,460 administrators.
- In the last three decades, the number of administrators and managers employed by American colleges and universities has ballooned, dwarfing the growth of student and faculty populations. From 1987 to 2012, colleges and universities across the country hired 517,636 administrators and professional employees—an average of 87 hires for every working day.
- The American Council of Trustees and Alumni (ACTA) found that, across the entire higher education landscape, spending on administration per student increased by 61 percent between 1993 and 2007.
- Presidents at both public and private universities often make comparable salaries to business executives of similar-sized institutions and receive extensive perks typically associated with corporate executives.
- Meanwhile, a report from the American Federation of Teachers found over 25 percent of adjunct faculty rely on public assistance and 40 percent struggle to cover basic costs, with nearly a third of those surveyed reporting making under $25,000—the federal poverty line.

In his article, Dinino quotes Benjamin Ginsberg's book *The Fall of the Faculty: The Rise of the All-Administrative University and Why It Matters*

Every year, hosts of administrators and staffers are added to college and university payrolls, even as schools claim to be battling budget crises that are forcing them to reduce the size of their full-time faculties. As a result, universities are filled with armies of functionaries—vice presidents, associate vice presidents, assistant vice presidents, provosts, associate provosts, assistant provosts, deans, deanlets, deanlings, each commanding staffers and assistants—who, more and more, direct operations of every school. Backed by their administrative legions, university presidents and other senior administrators have been able, at most schools, to dispense with faculty involvement in campus management and, thereby, reduce the faculty's influence in university affairs.

This level of spending is not surprising. Customers are told the product is mandatory and they can borrow endlessly, without repercussion, to purchase it. How many professors and administrators do you think have their paychecks connected to whether one of their students has gotten a good job? Administrators are rewarded for *enrollment*. Professors are rewarded for research and *recognition by the university*. The incentive plan is misaligned, the money is free, and no one is accountable for the outcome.

None of us is without blame. Like the social media crisis destroying the mental health of our youth, we all watched ballooning debt destroy the financial future of an entire generation and chose to look the other way. Four years after COVID-19, we are still trying to push repayment into some never-ending future or dispose of our responsibility entirely.

The jig is up, but higher education doesn't know it yet. Recent graduates are already struggling to find jobs that satisfy their expectations around salary and personal fulfillment. Employers report a significant mismatch in graduate skills in comparison to the skills needed. The market is facing a glut of political science and sociology majors, while we have a shortage of plumbers and truck drivers. Many young adults report being under-employed, taking jobs outside of their chosen field that often do not require the skills earned through their four-year degree. All of this was *before* the AI revolution.

The market for education will be much tougher in its selection process in the twenty-first century. We are all aware of prominent luminaries who never attended or finished college: Sam Altman of OpenAI, Mark Zuckerberg and Dustin Moskovitz of Facebook/Meta, Bill Gates and Paul Allen of Microsoft, Steve Jobs of Apple, and Travis Kalanick of Uber. Jack Dorsey of Twitter, Larry Ellison of Oracle, film icon Steven Spielberg, and shoe mogul Steve Madden. The list goes on and on. Few of the industrialists who built America had any formal education. When looking at some of the most successful people in history, it calls into question the need for higher education at all.

Am I suggesting that no one attend college? Not necessarily, but the twenty-first century will have a different version of the path to success. There will *always* be a need for great minds to gather. This is happening every day, all day long, outside of universities, thanks to the power of the internet. Teams meet and work through Zoom, Google Meet, and other platforms. Live streaming and podcasts are ubiquitous. Entire seminars are projected across the globe. Online communities share specialized knowledge in open forums.

THERE WILL *ALWAYS* BE A NEED FOR GREAT MINDS TO GATHER.

The high-level research opportunities I mentioned in chapter 3 are usually reserved for the brightest minds at the best universities. The majority of students will never see the opportunity to work on transformative medical breakthroughs or groundbreaking science in a university setting. In fact, quite the opposite is happening. We are seeing a rapid transition to innovation at speed. High-level students are dropping out in large numbers to join incubators and form their own companies. In 2025, the largest number of the rocket ship start-ups, that Wall Street and Silicon Valley call "unicorns," were formed by entrepreneurs in their early twenties. At the twenty-first-century pace, no one has time to wait.

What about the more traditional professions that require years of training, like doctors, lawyers, and scientists? We will still need some version of these. But AI will change everything. The accumulation of knowledge will be uprooted by the fact that knowledge is easily accessible at your fingertips. The emphasis will be on skills and training. For example, a medical student may complete their education online and then proceed directly to a hospital for hands-on training without ever stepping onto a university campus. If it can be done faster, cheaper, and more efficiently outside of the university system, it will be. New avenues will be developed to acquire any of the skills AI or robots can't do. For every aspect of a university-based education, an alternative route will be developed. Just look at the success of Khan Academy. With 170 million registered users across 190 countries, it's arguably the largest educational forum in the world.

Here is my bold prediction. Over the next ten years, you will begin to see a cascading overhaul of the current university system, looking something like this:

- As the white-collar and starter-level jobs that college graduates used to begin their careers with disappear, the value of a four-year education will drop dramatically.

- Enrollments will begin to drop in unison with the realization that spending four years and $100,000 plus will no longer guarantee a good job.
- As enrollment drops, colleges and universities will first be confronted with a financial crisis. Without the continual support of government-backed student debt filling their coffers, universities will no longer be able to sustain bloated bureaucracies and luxury amenities.
- Layoffs will begin with the excess administration, followed by the non-tenured professors. The layoffs will create fear in the master's and PhD classes, who would normally take these positions. As the illusion of a never-ending university lifestyle disappears, enrollment in graduate programs will begin to drop as well.
- Courses and degrees will be eliminated entirely due to a lack of qualified professors.
- As campuses begin to empty out, there will be a significant impact on the surrounding ecosystems that rely on the same government-backed student debt. Restaurants, services, apartment buildings, bars, and stores will all begin to feel the pinch.
- This vicious cycle will continue until the unbearable weight of finance eventually leads to the closing of many public institutions. Private universities will have their own crises.

The counter move to this will undoubtedly be the continued call for free public education. With the veil lifted, it's left to be seen whether taxpayers will willingly fund four expensive years on a university campus just for the sake of postponing the real world, especially when cheaper, faster alternatives are available. The tax base that would normally have to foot the bill will be worried about their own income and employment.

The cries for the wealthy to pay their fair share will result in the avoidance of taxes in every possible way. Private universities will see their endowments shrink. In the long run, it won't matter anyway. These are the things that happen in any great disruption. Old systems fall, and new systems rise.

Within any great change, there is always great opportunity.

WHAT DO WE DO NOW?

In a world where the twentieth-century idea of a job is no longer the objective, university-based education in a post-knowledge world loses its value. As the university degree loses its preeminent position as the primary driver of how and why children attend school, the entire scaffolding of "college begins in kindergarten" breaks down. With AI rapidly ascending, a whole new paradigm will define the twenty-first century. Here's the great news:

We have the opportunity to create a new system entirely built around children.

FIRST PRINCIPLES

First principles, initially attributed to Aristotle and often championed by luminaries like Elon Musk, are a problem-solving technique that involves breaking down complex issues into their most basic, fundamental truths, and then reassembling them from the ground up. It's about questioning assumptions and building understanding from the core components, rather than relying on conventional wisdom or analogy. It has four key elements:

1. Deconstruction: The process begins by breaking down a problem into its smallest, most fundamental parts.
2. Fundamental Truths: Identify the basic, undeniable truths or axioms upon which the problem is built.
3. Reconstruction: Rebuild the solution or understanding from these fundamental truths, rather than relying on established solutions or common practices.
4. Challenging Assumptions: Question existing assumptions and seek a deeper understanding of why things are the way they are.

In the sections above, we have deconstructed some of the problems of education and come to a universal truth: The system was never designed for the health and well-being of children; it was designed for production. Nowhere in the model was there an emphasis on creativity and imagination. If we were to use first-principles thinking, here are some of the goals we would imagine:

1. Get rid of twentieth-century thinking and the industrial model of education.
2. Throw out testing and university as the prime directives.
3. Adapt our thinking around their world in the twenty-first century.
4. Unleash a new generation of teachers, guides, and mentors trained for a different outcome.
5. Use the time gained to revert children back to imagination, play, and childhood.

First, we start with the assumption that there are no rules. We can approach this in so many different ways. As we move through the rest of this chapter, I want *every* parent, teacher, and caregiver to understand that this is a framework. My goal is to introduce a new world with options and tool sets, not tell you what to do.

Next, we want to create a North Star of our own in attempting to create a path for success. Sir Ken Robinson defined the purpose of education as the following:

> To empower individuals to understand the world around them and their own unique talents, enabling them to become fulfilled individuals and active, engaged citizens.[21]

That's pretty good! What a great North Star. Where I become incredibly optimistic is how that goal fits the opportunity in the twenty-first century. If jobs and universities aren't the main objective, we can focus our energy and efforts on the success of the individual. Creative Intelligence, as defined in this book, is the key to that objective.

HOW DO WE GO ABOUT CONSTRUCTING CREATIVE INTELLIGENCE?

Let's start by reframing our perspective. The modern war *within* education has created significant fragmentation. Parents and experts argue over the best environment for a child to learn. There's the traditional public school, private school, charter school, homeschooling, micro-schooling, and online schooling. The list goes on and on and grows longer each year. Except for some social aspects of human connection, which I will discuss later, I really don't care *where* a child spends their day. I believe every parent has the right to choose how they will raise their kids. What I do care about is the *environment* a child experiences. For the remainder of this chapter, I am going to replace the words *school* and *education* with the words *development environment.* That means the principles, framework, and techniques we create can be utilized regardless of location.

> **Secret # 6:** The levers that give us the power to transform a child's life during the development phase are *Time* and *Experience.*
>
> **Secret # 7:** Our role as parents, teachers, administrators, and caregivers is to provide *experiences* that create *patterns* frequently enough for them to become *habits* within the *time* we are allotted.

I know I gave you two secrets at once. Let's dig into the weight of both.

TIME

As I began chapter three, I expressed my opinion about the urgency and importance of hardwiring these patterns during the critical stages between five and ten years old. If we dig a little deeper, that gives us about six years. If we assume about two hundred full days per year within our development environment, we have approximately twelve hundred days to build wildly imaginative, capable, and healthy human beings. With focus, that's plenty of time. We'll go into even further below, but it's important to mention that I am not describing the *whole* picture of a child's life.

Healthy humans begin at birth. An abundance of literature and expertise describes what happens from the ages of one to five. For the most part, we do a good job of treating children like children during those years. Conversely, development doesn't end at ten or eleven. When a child enters adolescence, a new level of development begins, one more complex than the one we are discussing here. The brain starts a new reorganization process designed to fit the child's new challenges. There are world-renowned experts in these fields who are far more appropriate to read and reference regarding those stages. From my perspective, there are two major development phases after a child's earliest years:

5–10: During this phase, children should be focused exclusively on building Creative Intelligence through Exploration and Play.

11–20: Adolescents, until they reach early adulthood, should primarily focus on *aligning their purpose and values*. If we have done a good job of building Creative Intelligence, children should be well-prepared for this challenging stage, where they will figure out *who they are* and what they will *do* with the next one hundred years of their life. During this phase, children will take the power of the mental frameworks and skills they have developed and begin to apply them to the real world.

You can apply the techniques described in this book to toddlers through adults in various ways. I hope much of what we learn and discuss in our journey is adapted from cradle to grave. For now, we will focus on how we build patterns and habits at an early age that are meant to last a lifetime.

EXPERIENCE

If we go back to chapter two and the brain, you'll recall that our understanding of the world is built through a collection of experiences. Through every single experience we encounter from birth, our brain creates connections and patterns that form the foundation from which all thoughts and actions emerge. It then organizes these experiences into roadways and maps by strengthening meaningful connections and pruning what is not needed. The stronger the connection, the stronger the pattern, and the more likely it will become a habit. However, not all experiences are the same. The brain takes in so much information that it must prioritize, categorize, and organize experiences for access and later use. The more important the brain perceives an experience, the more likely it is to organize and label it for easy and rapid access. Both good and bad experiences can permanently impact the brain. That's why the foundations of imagination and creativity are so closely correlated with mental health. A child's experiences will affect them for the rest of their lives. It is paramount that the time a child spends within our development environment is *optimized* for experience.

> **WE NEED TO DEDICATE OUR TIME AND CURRICULA TO EXPERIENTIAL LEARNING.**

We need to dedicate our time and curricula to experiential learning. I'm talking immersive, thought-provoking, interactive, collaborative, and above all, *fun* experiences. The power of this environment is not solely its potential for learning. It's also about motivation. Speak to teachers in the classroom, and they will tell you that, under the current model, students are disengaged and disaffected. How do we expect them to learn and grow when they are not interested? We need to make them feel that coming to our environment is an event they don't want to miss. We want them dying to see what new adventure awaits them each day they rise. It sounds like a lot of pressure to put on the person leading the environment. But guess what? Teachers and administrators are burned out and disengaged with the current model too.

My prediction is that by freeing up parents, teachers, and administrators to create exciting, experience-filled days, we will reignite their passion for developing children. All of those young idealists who joined the profession believing they could impact a child's life will find their effort and commitment have purpose and value once again. The teaching profession, rather than flaming out, should become one of the most valuable professions in the world. Highly talented developmental leaders will be compensated according to that value in the same way that self-help authors are highly regarded and well-compensated for helping adults. In a jobless, post-university, high-speed, and complex world, *developing children for value and purpose is the most critical skill set.*

WHAT DOES OUR DEVELOPMENT ENVIRONMENT LOOK LIKE?

Before we dive into mechanics, we should discuss some extremely important topics that will have an enormous impact on the development environment. We'll start with Parents, Teachers, and Technology.

Technology

Let's talk tech. Similar to the arguments over which environment is best for children, an equally contentious disagreement is going on about the use of technology within the classroom. While technology companies and AI advocates calmly explain how everything in the world is better with technology, parents and educators, who have witnessed the damaging effects of improper use, are losing their minds over its impact and calling for it to be scrapped.

To gain clarity in this conversation, we must be brutally honest about how tech has affected our children. The conclusion is pretty much universal: we screwed up.

If you're a parent or educator and haven't yet read *The Anxious Generation* by Jonathan Haidt, you should probably pick it up the minute you put this book down. In the book, Haidt explores the connections between excessive smartphone use and the rise in mental health issues. In particular, he argues that screen time and social media have "shattered" attention spans, creating enormous problems in children's ability to focus, engage in meaningful interactions, build relationships, and develop crucial cognitive skills.[22]

In a recent article published by the *Financial Times,* journalist John Brun-Murdoch writes about a recent survey of young adults from sixteen to thirty-nine years of age. In their own words, they describe themselves as distracted, unable to follow through with plans, less outgoing, less talkative, less helpful, less conscientious, and more neurotic.[23]

These issues are not isolated to smartphones. The damage includes platforms like video games, tablets, and computers. Basically, screen time. There is a reason for the rise in calls for no-tech schools. Just ask a teacher, and they will tell you that none of these studies is a surprise. They see it live every day. We have lost an entire generation mentally, and there's no certainty we'll ever get them back.

Whose fault is this? There's plenty of blame to go around. When Steve Jobs invented the iPhone, his intention was to open us up to a world of possibilities. I doubt he had the vision of entire populations, head down, necks craning, posture fading for fourteen hours a day watching selfies and influencers. Not long after the introduction of the iPhone, tech companies began a long train of developing apps built around addiction models. The entire goal of these apps is to get people *addicted* to watching. Boy, did they succeed. These platforms are so powerful that old tobacco companies only dreamed of the plethora of addicts being created. We have known about this for a long time now, and yet, what have we done about it? In the old days, we sued and prosecuted tobacco companies for their intentional poisoning of people for profit. In the tech era, we have responded by signing up for more apps. As a society, we didn't just let the wolves through the door; we invited them in.

In response to his research, Haidt advocates for what he calls the four norms:

- No smartphone until age fourteen
- No social media before sixteen
- Phone-free schools
- More independence, free play, and responsibility in the real world

I am all-in on the Haidt train, but what about other tech in schools? Similarly, we have failed our children. When the idea of introducing technology into schools came about, it was sold as a way to *improve* education. No doubt, a computer may have enhanced the learning environment in some ways. Once again, however, we didn't handle it responsibly. Children are now surrounded by an overabundance of tech while in school. Many have their own cell phones. Classes and lessons are taught entirely on tablets and computers. Teachers and parents alike admit to very little *schoolwork* being done. Children have full access to the internet, social media, video gaming, chatting, and texting. Even lessons are *gamified* for maximum dopamine hits. Statistics show that technology has done little to improve learning, but everyone knows what kind of damage it has done to our children.

What is so crazy is that most of the tech luminaries who create these models don't let their own kids use them. Mark Zuckerberg, Bill Gates, Steve Jobs, and many of the Silicon Valley elite keep technology away from their kids at an early age. Zuckerberg and Elon Musk went as far as creating schools for their children.

AI has the potential to scale this lunacy ten times. A recent study at MIT's Media Lab studied the effects of its participants using AI for writing tasks vs those who wrote without AI assistance. The study measured brain activity using an EEG. Its findings were a huge warning:

Those who relied heavily on AI to write their papers showed lower cognitive engagement, poorer memory recall, and a diminished sense of ownership. Many students could not recall a single sentence from the paper they just turned in. Imaging revealed weak activity in the frontal and parietal lobes, along with highly reduced connectivity. Conversely, those who first wrote the papers on their own and then later revised with AI showed higher brain activity and connectivity, as well as better memory and recall.

In summary, the results showed that "cognitive offloading," allowing the machine to do the thinking for you, resulted in "cognitive debt"—the inability to perform the same tasks at the same level later. As with social media and the smartphone, we have generally adapted our initial use of AI platforms like ChatGPT to replace thinking. Replacing our thinking is the death of all our most valuable human characteristics. Forget imagination and creativity.

With all of the negative consequences discussed above, it might surprise you that I am an advocate for the possibilities of using AI in the development environment. Let me share the reasons why:

1. **It's their world.** As I discussed in the opening chapter of this book, AI is here to stay. It will be a part of everyday life in hundreds of ways by the time our children reach adulthood. If we do not actively teach AI literacy and application to our children, they will be left behind in a world designed for it.

2. **Mastery, Progression, and Individualized Learning.** This is not your father's tech. A major fault line in the industrial model has always been a one-size-fits-all approach to learning. Research has repeatedly shown that all individuals develop at different rates in unique ways. Most of the technology developed in the 80s, 90s, and early 2000s was developed with the general approach in mind. Create a product that has as many features as possible to be used by the greatest number of people. Dropping a misaligned product into a poorly designed system and then ignoring how it was being used or abused is a perfect trifecta for a bad outcome.
Education advocates have long been crying for a program that prioritizes individual learning. The latest versions of AI-powered learning platforms were *designed* with individualized learning in mind. These systems work off new models of *Mastery* and *Progression*. A student is taught a lesson, and at the same time, challenged to show that they have mastered the

subject matter. If the student has not been able to show mastery, they do not advance to the next lesson. The system tracks the student's progression automatically and notifies the teacher of any issues. If a student is struggling to master a subject, the teacher steps in and has the responsibility for understanding why learning has stalled. On the other hand, if a student is succeeding with lessons in quick order, he or she is allowed to progress as fast and as high as possible. No need to stop and wait for test scores; the system monitors the effectiveness of each student's learning path. No one needs to wait for the entire class to catch up; students are allowed to progress at a pace that makes sense for them. We can now create environments where every child has access to their individual path.

Low floors, high ceilings, and wide walls

One of my favorite books on creativity is *Lifelong Kindergarten* by Mitchel Resnick. Resnick is a professor of research at the MIT Media Lab and founder of the Lab's Lifelong Kindergarten group. He has spent more than thirty years studying children and creativity. He and his associate, Natalie Rusk, created SCRATCH, a programming language for kids to explore creativity through technology, and Computer Clubhouse, an international network of more than a hundred after-school learning centers where youth from low-income communities learn to express themselves creatively. Resnick also collaborated with the LEGO company on developing the LEGO Mindstorms robotics kits. So yes, I highly recommend this book.

I wanted to mention this important concept from the book. Children need broad learning environments and experiences to develop creatively and maximize their potential. In the connections between creativity and technology, Resnick developed a framework I admire for maximizing the value of individualized learning:

> **Low Floors:** We need to give every child the opportunity to start from where they are currently capable and work up from there.
>
> **High Ceilings:** We need to ensure that bright minds can soar as high and as fast as they can without constraint.
>
> **Wide Walls:** We need to provide the widest possible number of approaches and pathways to learning, as all children learn differently and are motivated by different interests.

3. **Foundational Learning.** From an academic perspective, AI will change the world of knowledge. That means children will not have to memorize a whole array of facts, figures, and information they might never use. But that doesn't mean they don't need to build foundational knowledge. We'll use STEM as an example.

   For the last decade, as nations, states, and school boards have attempted to align the job markets with education, significant emphasis has been placed on learning fields such as *Science, Technology, Engineering, and Math*. As with most initiatives, the intention was good. While the rest of a child's development may have taken a back seat, educators were trying to ensure that children could participate in the economy they were entering. Not every child will need to learn high levels of any of these categories in the future. However, should they *choose* to pursue these fields, they will need a strong foundation and thorough understanding of the major concepts and principles if they hope to effectively use or manage AI. All children will need to have a solid foundation in reading comprehension and basic math. We should also include an elementary understanding of science, geography, and history. For example, a child who dreams of constructing beautiful buildings might need a solid base in math, engineering, and architecture, even if AI will do much of the heavy lifting.

As we move to experiential learning environments, we'll need to make sure there are mechanisms to ensure children have the right foundational knowledge to build upon. As I will discuss in the next section, AI is a powerful tool in ensuring that outcome.

4. **Time.** Time is our most precious gift. We only have so many days and hours to prepare our children for the world they will inherit. The greatest impact that AI can have on the development environment is to give us back time. If we are going to build the correct wiring and mental frameworks for Creative Intelligence, we need to flip the model upside down and reserve the most time for experiential learning. The primary obstacle to that form of learning in current environments has been the radical approach of chaining children to desks for

eight hours a day and trying to test them into a head full of facts. No time for imagination, no time for play, no time for personal interests. One of the promises of AI is a dramatic increase in learning *efficiency*.

2-hour learning

Don't let anybody tell you people aren't innovating in education. There are a number of innovative organizations and innovative companies attempting to revolutionize the learning environment. It just may not be *your school* or *your school district*. Without advocating for any one approach or AI platform, I wanted to share an organization that is gaining a lot of attention—the Alpha School—which promotes itself as an AI-powered private school. Mackenzie Price, the founder of Alpha School, recreated the learning environment using a platform called 2-Hour Learning, where students use a two-hour block of time each morning to tackle academics, reserving the entire afternoon for skills-based exploration and learning. You can imagine my excitement for this approach. If we can tackle *foundational* learning in two hours and leave a large portion of the day for *experiential* learning, we unlock the key to developing intelligent, imaginative, creative, and mentally healthy children.

The results currently being touted by the group are impressive. With just two hours of AI-based academic instruction, primary and middle schoolers are, on average, learning at least 2X faster than their peers in traditional models, completing entire grades in half the time. Top performers are recording a pace at 4X normal learning curves. High Schoolers' average SAT scores of 1470. Students overall are performing in the ninety-ninth percentile of national testing. Moreover, by limiting the more restrictive part of sitting in front of a computer to just two hours, students are more engaged, more motivated, and happier throughout the day.

These environments don't necessarily fit every child, and it will take a lot of work to transform these models into one that works in larger classrooms and school systems. What it does show, however, is that utilizing AI can drive a more efficient academic environment, leaving plenty of *time* to develop Creative Intelligence. This is how we take back our childhood and ensure appropriate levels of knowledge for properly functioning in the real world.

> **BY LIMITING THE MORE RESTRICTIVE PART OF SITTING IN FRONT OF A COMPUTER TO JUST TWO HOURS, STUDENTS ARE MORE ENGAGED, MORE MOTIVATED, AND HAPPIER THROUGHOUT THE DAY.**

5. **Opportunity to level the playing field.** This may be the most important reason of all. For the first time in history, we have a real opportunity to level the playing field for all children around the world. If executed properly, Artificial Intelligence, used in combination with experiential learning, can create a scenario where children in rural Arkansas or a district in Mumbai have access to exactly the same development environment as a child in the most elite section of Manhattan. AI solves the academic portion. Platforms like Khan Academy and its AI-powered teaching assistant, Khanmigo, can teach all forms of knowledge up to the highest levels

of university-based PhD-level courses. Every teacher on the planet can learn to adopt a creative, explorative environment. The only thing that keeps us from achieving this incredible milestone for humanity is the willingness to make it a priority.

Am I advocating for turning over our children to the immense power of Artificial Intelligence? Of course not. What I am advocating for is limited, focused, and purposeful use of AI platforms to tackle the academic portion of development. When we eliminate the idea that children must be filled with facts, we reduce the time needed for memorized learning. When we eliminate the idea of teachers being responsible for delivering testing results and reframe them as leaders in the development environment, the *availability of time* and the *efficiency of learning* will be essential in maximizing outcomes.

It's time for us to take ownership of our own actions, or lack thereof. If our children are going to successfully navigate a world driven by AI, they must learn how to use it responsibly. Instead of just relying on technology to do it for us, we need to operate on a set of basic guidelines:

1. The use of technology and AI should never be utilized to replace thinking.
2. Technology should be seen as a tool set to enhance our foundational capabilities and break through any limitations of our own natural intelligence.
3. Academic Learning in early environments should take a back seat to the development of Creative Intelligence.

TEACHERS

I'd like to make an announcement: I am a HUGE advocate for great teachers. A great teacher is a gift to humanity. A kind and competent teacher is one of the most powerful tools in society's arsenal. A true connection with a single teacher can change the entire trajectory of a child's life.

At times, teaching sounds like the worst profession in the world. Students won't pay attention, and all are addicted to their cell phones. Parents are constantly angry about a grade, the actions of another child, or their own child's performance. The government, the school board, and the administration tie your hands. You are seen as service workers responsible for delivering standards, or worse, educated babysitters. Regardless of the outcome, you are to blame for everything that happens to the children under your care. Why would anyone on earth want to be a teacher?

For the critics, a teacher is a *person* like the rest of us. There are terrible teachers, there are great teachers, and the rest are somewhere in between, just like every other profession on earth. You think every accountant is a great accountant? Every doctor is a stellar doctor? Is every lawyer, cop, construction worker, nurse, programmer, cook, or dishwasher at their best every day of the week? If we are honest, most of us are somewhere in the middle. That's the very reason we can describe what being terrible or being great looks like. Because teachers take care of our children, we expect them to provide concierge service at the highest levels day in and day out without fail. That's a pretty tall order. Ask yourself how you would do if you were held to that standard at your job. I'm not saying there aren't some pretty bad ones. And I don't want to get involved with some of the politics causing great divides. I don't think politics belong in the classroom. Period. What I am saying is, what would we do without teachers?

Let's look at some options. Regarding public schools, we currently hand over our kids to government rules and conformity, and hope teachers do a good job. With a private school, you pay for other people to develop your kids, and hope they do a good job. If you are homeschooling, you take on that responsibility. There are positives and negatives to all of these environments and approaches. None of us knows exactly what the AI-driven world will look like in twenty-plus years. Will we still have mass education? Who pays for that in a jobless world? Will people who still have jobs send their kids to private school? If parents who don't have jobs sit at home all day, will they be required to handle the schooling responsibility on their own? Do we think *all* parents will make good teachers? Our social media crises might provide a clue. What if parents don't want to teach? What if they want to spend their days pursuing their own interests, their own purpose, or a life of luxury promised by the abundance of AI? Do we leave development up to robots? If we remove government and standards from the equation and call it a free-for-all, what does education look like then? Do you think we might have some bad outcomes?

> **NONE OF US KNOWS EXACTLY WHAT THE AI-DRIVEN WORLD WILL LOOK LIKE IN TWENTY-PLUS YEARS.**

When we devalue the need for great teachers, we dismiss the training and effort that goes into the profession and overvalue our own competencies and capabilities. I like to use a fireman analogy when I think about who will lead future development environments.

All of us can put out a small fire. We know how to throw water on a campfire, throw a towel over a small kitchen fire, or stomp on a book of matches. But what about a raging fire? Would you trust your own skills if your child were trapped in a fourteen-story building burning from the ground up? What if none of your teammates were trained in how to operate the truck, turn on the pumps, put on protective gear, raise the ladder, or safely enter the building?

If we flip the script in an AI world and focus on experience-based learning, we will need more teachers than ever. There are many aspects of Creative Intelligence that AI can't teach, most of all human connection. We will need highly trained and skilled teachers to lead exciting, immersive, and fun environments. We need to get rid of bad teachers, help good teachers become great teachers, and do everything we can to keep great teachers from leaving the profession.

One last bit. Ask yourself what you prefer for your child: a person who loves and cares for them, who also knows how to connect intimately and optimize their experience? Or instruction primarily through screens or robots, or worse, children left entirely alone to their own devices?

PARENTS

The idea of keeping parents out of classrooms is insanity to me. Research consistently shows that parental involvement enormously impacts development outcomes. Setting aside the issue of helicopter parenting or other forms of over-involvement, having parents involved and engaged in their children's development improves social development, emotional development, classroom behavior, test performance, grades, and graduation rates, in addition to motivation, resilience, and attitude toward learning.

Quite the opposite happens when parents are disengaged. Students show up to class unprepared, unmotivated, distracted, and disengaged. In such cases, learning isn't an option. Students quit before they step through the door. Even those who want to learn can find themselves isolated and without help or guidance. Nearly everything leading to success begins in the home.

We want parents involved. In a development environment outside the home, the best possible set-up for a child is a true partnership between the parents and the teacher. If parents care about their child's education, the child is much more likely to care for themselves. If parents are excited about learning and school, the child, too, is more likely to be excited. If the parent is interested in what is being taught, the child is much more likely to be interested. The parents' engagement in the process is the most significant indicator to children that education matters and that the children themselves are important.

Any great system will be designed to support the parents and teachers in the best interest of the child.

Skills and traits

Let's take a moment and go back to some of the goals of a powerful development environment.

Top Five Skills

1. Imagination and creativity
2. Adaptability, flexibility, and resilience
3. Curiosity and intrinsic motivation
4. Critical thinking and problem-solving
5. Collaboration and communication

Top Traits

1. Positive self-esteem
2. An empowered psychology based in possibilities
3. A love of exploration and learning
4. A bias toward action
5. An orientation toward goals and objectives
6. Comfort with ambiguity and risk-taking
7. The desire to seek alternatives
8. Comfort with failure

Man, that's a lot to accomplish. But wait! We're not done yet. If we hope to develop productive, engaged citizens, we'll also want to include things like kindness, compassion, empathy, and human connection. Seems like a lot to take on. Worry not. This is where the Wylde Method and Wylde Loop come in. By following these frameworks, everything listed above is baked in. I'll explain as we move along.

GUIDEPOSTS

Creators Create

> *The real work of the artists is a way of being in the world.*
>
> —Rick Rubin, *The Creative Act*

One of the primary themes I took away from Resnick's *Lifelong Kindergarten* was that if we want children to learn how to create, we must give them numerous and repeated opportunities to create something from scratch. For a long time, my thought process was focused primarily on the idea of how we build bright, beautiful imaginations. As I began to incorporate the impacts of AI and the twenty-first-century transformation, the "create" in Creative Intelligence began to rival the importance of ideas. Imagination only has one advantage over creativity in that it stands as its predecessor. But if we fail to execute on those ideas, they become less relevant. Thankfully, the Wylde loops contain the capacity to build both. Rather than controlling the entire day, as we have in the past, we need to remember to stand back and let children work things out on their own if they are to perform independently. Imagine, at the core of our children, a connection between joy and creativity, the state of happiness being connected to the act of creation.

Gravity and natural acceleration

The future has little need for followers. The robots will do that well. If you remember my AA battery analogy in chapter 1, the launch power in the real world will be children who are intrinsically motivated, endlessly curious, and capable of learning on their own. If we have done a good job in the development environment, we will have created a generation of children who can think on their own, create ideas on their own, discover what interests them, explore those interests, and follow these paths to finding purpose and delivering value to the wider world. Most good caregivers have a strong desire to guide children. Of course, parents and teachers are supposed to serve as guides. But like the discussion above on creativity, we need to ensure that, within the environment, the children have time to discover and pursue their natural interests. Frankly, I am astonished at the continual question of how to *motivate* students. Children will *gravitate* toward whatever makes them happy. If you understand the deepest nature of intrinsic motivation, people, by nature, will pursue things that they connect with. They will try harder, work longer, and suffer failures far more for things they care about. Without time for exploration, children will find it more difficult to find their right path. This path will be the key to *purpose* and *value,* the very currencies of the AI-driven world.

Sir Ken Robinson quotes educator Jerry Minz in his book: "If you force kids to learn things they are not interested in over seven or eight years, after a while you extinguish that natural ability to learn."[24]

I am going to make another prediction about the future of education. Today, when someone is considered a true genius, society lets them step outside the bounds of traditional education. Hyper-intelligent individuals are allowed to accelerate at their own speed. We have all heard about young mathematicians heading to MIT at sixteen or other remarkable individuals graduating from medical school before their eighteenth birthday. Once we strip away the idea that everyone is in search of a job and requires perfect SAT scores to maximize their chances at a four-year degree from the right university, accelerated paths become the norm.

Empowered children will dictate their own path and speed. Once they have reached a certain degree of foundational frameworks and autonomous thinking, they will use these capabilities to pursue the end goal of healthy participation in the real world. There's no guarantee that anyone will remain within a protected learning environment all the way to eighteen, and why should they? Some may head off to specialized university-level training at a young age. Others may join a scientific lab at fourteen. Another might join an entrepreneurial incubator at fifteen. And there will be those who have a fully functioning business with robots, employees, and a million customers by sixteen. Some will decide they are happiest fixing robots. It doesn't really matter what they do. If they have made the decision and acquired the skills to be successful, we have gone a long way in solving the great question of purpose and value in the twenty-first century. Our responsibility in the early years of development is to ingrain this type of thinking into their very mindset.

> **EMPOWERED CHILDREN WILL DICTATE THEIR OWN PATH AND SPEED.**

Chapter 7

THE WYLDE ENVIRONMENT

Now we're finally getting to the nitty-gritty. Let's start with the structure of a successful development environment and then dig into the mechanics.

In addition to being an endless optimist, I'm a practical thinker. I like to dream about possibilities, then try to figure out how that works in the real world. The starting point for any child is the basic twenty-four-hour clock we all use to manage our day.

If you think about our customary routines, a child's day may look something like this:

Rise early.

Get dressed in a fog.

Stare into the phone while quickly eating breakfast.

Stare into the phone on the bus.

Sit for eight hours at one desk or many desks with a couple of brief breaks.

Check the phone as often as possible.

Listen to uninteresting lectures or struggle through mind-numbing, task-oriented exercises.

Pray the day ends soon.

Get back on the bus and stare into the phone.

Land at home.

Spend two hours on the phone or playing video games until it's time to eat dinner.

Maybe some homework in between.

Back to video games or a cell phone in bed until falling asleep.

We're talking about a child's day, but we could easily switch out the word *school* for *work* and end up describing the typical day for many adults. If we all continue down this path, we are guaranteed an outcome like the one I described in the movie *WALL-E*. Or perhaps worse, a real-life version of the movie *Idiocracy*. We may survive, but mental health will continue to decline, and everyone will struggle with purpose and value.

If we want a different outcome, we have to completely revamp how we spend the day. First, let's talk about *Time*. For parents, I want to emphasize that every minute of the day counts. There are a million ways in which you can contribute to your child's development and mindset from the moment they wake up. I'll give examples below. For parents who choose to homeschool, you may have the entirety of the day to mix it up. You have ample opportunity to accomplish everything you need with intention. For teachers, you might have children under your care for a total of about six and a half hours per day. We'll discuss how to optimize that opportunity. As pragmatists, let's break down the reality of available time.

We'll start by taking twelve hours off the top for sleep and standard family routines like showering, eating, bedtime routines, and so on. That leaves us with about twelve hours to be concerned with development. Typically, much of this time is consumed by travel and other life necessities, so we'll discuss some basic guidelines for what I call *the structured day*—the available eight-hour block between 8 a.m. and 4 p.m. Traditionally, we call this the typical school day. I want *everyone* to believe that they are capable of changing a child's life within these parameters. I don't believe in any way that every family, parent, child, school, and teacher needs to operate in the same way for these outcomes. These are frameworks to be utilized in the best possible manner.

At the highest level, here is what a typical day might look like in implementing a Wylde environment.

Morning routine:

At home, all parents should start with Imagination Prompts and Positive Affirmations.

- Prompts: What did you dream about last night?
- Positive affirmations: Today is going to be the best day ever!
- Ride to school: open discussion about the approaching day.

You will notice there is NO CELL PHONE in this routine. If you want to kill curiosity, motivation, imagination, and creativity, start the day with a cell phone. You will erase all chances of creating active, vibrant minds before the day's begun.

Schooltime routine:

We are going to assume that in formal school environments, there will be requirements around academic learning and normal routines for transitions, lunch, and teacher prep. We will also assume that no two classrooms or environments will ever be alike. If we are ever going to transform the environment for the purpose of Creative Intelligence, we have to flip the school day to provide the majority of time for experience-based learning and limit time for academic progression. In our model, we will allow for a two-hour window we believe will suffice for core academics utilizing AI and individual-driven curricula. A typical day in a Wylde development environment might look like this:

1. Morning routine: 30 minutes
   a. Teacher Welcome
   b. Physical ignition (Stretch/Japanese style exercise, etc.)
   c. Prep routine for focused effort
2. Give them the basics; allow for 2-hour learning blocks.
   a. AI: Math/Science/Literacy/Civics/History
   b. Individualized Mastery and Progression
3. Lunch: 30 minutes
4. Free Unstructured Play: outside, 1 Hour
5. Imagination Prompt: 5 minutes
6. Silent Rest/Free thinking: 10 minutes
7. Project/Hands-On Time: 45 Minutes
   a. Alternate between Individual and Team Projects
8. Free Reading/Writing Time: Alternate after 30 minutes
9. Input Time- Exploration: 30 minutes
   a. Alternate: Arts/Music/Languages/Culture/History
10. Structured/unstructured Play Indoors: 30 minutes
    a. Teacher-Led Activities: Fun with Skills Building
    b. Memory Games
    c. Board Games at the table

PUZZLES

You will notice a few things here. Evidence has shown that children's attention is at its peak in the morning, so focused learning in academics should happen during that time. The 2-Hour learning program I described at the Alpha School is based on the Pomodoro technique, which breaks learning into focused, twenty-five-minute blocks to avoid boredom and burnout. In addition, I believe in physically engaging students through routines and rituals to prepare their minds for focused learning. A good example might be the way NBA players move around the court and take shots at the basket before a game begins, or Lebron James' ritual of rubbing his hands in chalk and clapping a big cloud before stepping onto the court.

While it's difficult to say exactly what type of academic learning will be required or needed as we move into the future, there is no doubt that deep focus is a requirement for Creative Intelligence and the Wylde Loops and Method. Helping children build upon intrinsic motivation and their own interests will drive their own penchant for deep focus, but in the early years, it will be important to build these habits and routines through repetitive patterns. It is good to have some period or periods throughout the day where deep focus is a normal part of the routine. By eliminating excessive time sitting at a desk, we are working to strike the right balance between focus and play.

Next, you will notice that for all children, a lunch break is necessary and routine. My real focus here is that *after* a child has spent time *sitting*, after *refueling* them, we need to release them into the wild. All children need to play. We will dive deeper into that below. If you want them focused on anything you do in the afternoon, some form of play must happen in the first half of the day.

That leaves us with somewhere in the neighborhood of four hours to really blow their minds. As you can see above, the afternoon is designed to be a mix of experiences. No two days need ever be the same. In fact, the mind demands variety. Building the most robust connections requires exposure to many different things. The best way we can do that is to provide and rotate a variety of experiences. That's where the Wylde Method comes into play. Through the different aspects of the Wylde Loops, we will be using the available time to create experiences that run the circle between focused modes and imaginative modes. Much of it should be based on exploration. By repeating different versions of the Loop, day in and day out, through varied experiences, we begin to develop the patterns and habits of Creative Intelligence.

> **BUILDING THE MOST ROBUST CONNECTIONS REQUIRES EXPOSURE TO MANY DIFFERENT THINGS. THE BEST WAY WE CAN DO THAT IS TO PROVIDE AND ROTATE A VARIETY OF EXPERIENCES.**

Developing these patterns and habits is where teachers have the opportunity to really shine. I've heard a lot of denigration of teachers based on the performance of the traditional education models. They say a teacher standing in front of a classroom doesn't work anymore. I agree; if all you want out of teachers is for them to regurgitate monotonous information for testing and retesting, then yes, you have wasted a generation of teachers. But the purpose of a true teacher is to lead in the development of a child. We want great teachers in the development environment. A "guide" by any other name is a teacher. If we hand teachers the freedom and tool sets to create exciting classrooms full of varied experiences, anything is possible. I'm repeating myself, but I really think we should *set great teachers free*.

Let's finish this section off by talking about what happens *after school*.

Evening routine:

I can hear the cheers from parents and children everywhere.... *No homework ever!* Yes, I believe that. Many innovative schools and programs have successfully removed homework from the daily routine and yet have kept standards of academic achievement at high levels. The reality of homework as an institution was created by pursuing a strategy of asking students to retain and memorize too much knowledge that they will never use. The only exceptions for me are projects that involve time with the parent or self-driven exploration; however, these projects should be limited in time and scope during the development phase. So what should families be doing with *home time*?

- Physical, outside, unstructured play: at least one hour
  - As an alternative, we know that many children will pursue other forms of physical or artistic activities, such as team sports, dance, or music lessons. Parents need to be cognizant of overscheduling children during the sensitive development years of 5–10 years old. They don't need it. There will be plenty of time to pick up hobbies and activities as they move along and discover interests they really want to pursue.

- Dinner/Family/Parent/Sibling Interaction Time: one hour
  - All families need to communicate. All children need time with attentive parents. All siblings need time to interact and play together. Please *put down the phone.* No phones should be at the dinner table. No parent should be distracted by the dinging of texts when their child is attempting to interact. And yes, I believe in the old-fashioned routine of a family sitting down for dinner and talking whenever possible. If you wonder where we've lost the battle against anxiety, depression, and loneliness? This is a good place to start.

- Pure Down Time/Mental Escape: thirty minutes

    Everyone needs a break. One of the great secrets of the imagination and baked into the Wylde Loop is the relaxation of the mind. If you truly want an active, explorative, agile, and responsive brain, you must rest it from time to time. Burnout is one of the main ingredients for mental blocks, not to mention mental health problems. I believe that there should be time at home for whatever makes people happy:

    - Favorite TV show
    - Favorite/Safe Video Game
    - Call with a friend

    This might surprise you, but I even believe in junk food for the brain, as long as it is safe, harmless, and monitored. That includes picking up a cell phone for a few minutes of relaxation.

- Bedtime Routine: one hour

    The worst thing you can do to a young child is send them off to their room alone with a cell phone in their hand, hoping they will fall asleep. Structured bedtime routines are important for the development of patterns and proper sleep cycles. After the physical prep of perhaps a bath, changing into pajamas, and brushing teeth, bedtime is truly one of the greatest opportunities for connection and development.

    The best thing you can ever do at night is to read a book with your child. A lot of parents do a good job of this until about five years old, but somewhere along the line, we forget how magical this time is and begin to shout commandments from down the hall or downstairs. "Go to bed!" "Light's out!", or "Don't make me come up there!" Like all things with children and the imagination, I have never understood why we cut this off this routine so early. A bedtime routine with an engaged parent should continue all the way through these important developmental years. You should already *be* up there. You should *stay* up there until the voices of early adolescence drive them to kick you out.

From a social and emotional standpoint, this opportunity for connection helps you bond with your child and gives you deep credibility when your child is navigating the world and *needs* input from someone they trust. From a Creative Intelligence perspective, there is no greater way to inspire the imagination. Thousands of age-appropriate books are available to read with your child. Thousands of worlds to explore. Think about what it does to a young child's imagination when you send them to sleep at night with story after story, after story. The benefits go even further if you have your child read books to you. Their confidence and self-esteem rise, their reading skills and comprehension improve, and they begin to develop strong language and verbal skills. All from thirty minutes lying down. What better return could you ask for in parent-child investment?

THE WYLDE LOOP IN PRACTICE

To put the whole picture together, we'll walk through the aspects of the Wylde Loop and discuss how the different aspects connect to and develop the core skills, traits, and habits of Creative Intelligence. Remember that time is limited, so we have no expectation that every activity will be included every day. The goal is to maximize these experiences as much as possible within the time available for development.

REST

What we do when we step away from the active pursuit of learning.

Reading and writing: bring back the book, paper, and pencil!

Reading

Reading is fundamental. To me, all other forms of learning extend from reading. Gutenberg's printing press was invented in 1440, spreading knowledge throughout the world, spawning the beginnings of the Enlightenment, and inspiring countless innovations. How we struggle with reading nearly six hundred years later befuddles me. If a child can't read, all other forms of academic learning should stop, and all our energy should be dedicated to figuring out how to help the child conquer that skill. I understand that learning by "doing" is an extremely powerful tool, but it is limited to the physical world around us.

Research has shown that reading physical books is better than looking at screens for a variety of reasons. Books produce deeper comprehension, better recall, and more critical thinking than screens. Studies show that books activate more brain activity and emotion than screens. Deep reading creates a slower, more thorough process than scrolling, improving complex understanding, while digital media has shown a more shallow processing of critical information.

But there's more to it. There's *Imagination*. How else does a six-year-old begin to travel the world and see places like Hogwarts, Narnia, the Hundred-Acre Wood, the Chocolate Factory, and Never-Never Land? How else does a five-year-old meet dragons and trolls, fairies and mermaids, or pirates and Lost Boys? How else can an eight-year-old go on wild, dangerous, and exciting adventures without ever leaving the safety of home or risking life and limb?

When a child reads, their brain does more than just receive information. Unlike the fragmented mess of scrolling or even the wonderful beauty of a richly animated film, when a child reads, their mind *creates*. Their brains translate black letters on a white page into something tangible and real. The word *castle* in a book is a collection of six random, boring letters—c-a-s-t-l-e—but in a child's mind, the options are unlimited. An image begins to take form and function: Large or small? Turrets? Iron Gates? Is there a princess inside? A king? Are there knights standing guard in the high towers? When they read those six letters, or hear their parents' words hang in the air, a child's imagination constructs the castle. They are training, practicing, rehearsing, and building connections.

Writing

> *In the process of writing, you learn to organize, refine, and reflect on your ideas. As you become a better writer, you become a better thinker.*
>
> —Mitch Resnick, *Lifelong Learning*

A similar process happens within the brain when writing. For a child to write something on a page, the brain has to activate and engage. It searches its endless database for ideas and information. It's forced to recall and utilize its memory. It can choose to regurgitate or create. Again, the brain is training, practicing, rehearsing, and building connections.

If you think that reading and writing don't sound like rest, watch what happens when you put a book in your child's hand, or send them to a table with nothing more than crayons, pencils, and blank paper. The objective is calm relaxation.

Yet reading and writing aren't the only ways children can learn. Play is an important factor too.

Play, play, and more play

Whoever thought growing up was a good idea? For all of us, true happiness fades when we stop playing. Just look at the people and world around you. What is a life focused only on *income*, *obligation*, and *material acquisition*? If you want to know why so many adults are *unhappy* or on prescription meds for anxiety and depression, ask them how much time in their life is allocated to play. The happiest among us have found a way to incorporate play into their daily purpose, routines, and lives.

A mountain of research backs up the critical importance of play in a child's life, and I don't want to simply repeat what is already being widely discussed. Groups all over the world advocate for the return of play. I'm in. I'm all-in. I'm overly in, as far as you can go.

We totally messed up when we decided it was a good idea to start stapling down children as young as five for long periods of the day. It goes against every natural process of development for a child and is the primary reason for the steep rise of ADHD, anxiety, and depression. Children need to play—a lot! They need to run, dispose of energy, interact with other children, laugh, make up games, challenge each other, and think for themselves. *All* research shows that play is essential for children's healthy development. Play enhances an unbelievable amount of vital development. It *stimulates neural connections* and improves *language and motor skills*. Play *fosters independence,* and it enhances *critical thinking, problem-solving, emotional regulation,* and *social skills.* It enhances *adaptability, flexibility,* and *collaboration.* Play allows for *exercise of the body, mind,* and *creativity.*

Most importantly, *play is the most natural way that young children learn.* There are basically three forms of play: *Unstructured Play, Structured Play,* and *Imaginative Play.* We'll save Structured Play for the next section.

UNSTRUCTURED PLAY

What is unstructured play? Exactly what it sounds like. We don't set the rules; the children do. The most common form is what we might associate with recess at school. Even that can be unintentionally turned into structured play through a well-intentioned coach. Although we don't want to confuse the idea with being unsupervised, the goal is as little interference as possible.

Children need to burn energy. They need to make choices. They need to build friendships. They need to fall down and get hurt. They need to invent games and create their own rules. They need to climb trees and explore. They need to take risks. They need to learn to solve problems on their own. All of this is a natural part of healthy development. While I understand we may never go back to the days of kids wandering miles from home on their bikes for twelve hours a day, we need to create as much freedom as possible, and they need to do this without our intervention every five minutes to assure ourselves that everything is okay.

Imaginative play

Can we develop a highly imaginative child who doesn't know what to do whenever adults stop managing their day? No. Tired, overscheduled, and overly managed children don't develop the ability to think independently, daydream, or invent. This is where the call to "let them be bored" comes in. When children are very young, this process occurs naturally. Toddlers roll around the semi-safety of the home or backyard and babble incoherently as they explore the world around them. Eventually, this exploration turns into mimicking, and soon they begin to pretend while playing. At a certain point, we are pretty good at joining them for pretend tea parties, cooking with fake pots and pans, and making zoom noises as we roll cars across the floor. Children are exceptionally capable of using their imagination to fill time in their day and gaps in their knowledge.

Often, our parental instincts and concerns disrupt the necessary patterns. We are overly concerned with whether or not they are bored. If they complain or cry after five minutes with "nothing to do," we begin to look for solutions. At the very worst end of the spectrum, we have learned to hand them a cell phone or a tablet to calm them down or entertain them—an effort to give us a moment while we focus on other things. When we do this, we are unintentionally killing their creative instincts. We have lots of ways to encourage imagination and prompt exercises in structured environments, but nothing is more powerful in developing creative intelligence during the early years than giving children time alone or with friends, with nothing but their imaginations to keep them occupied.

Children need a minimum of two to three hours per day of unstructured play. In addition to the enormous development value it brings on its own, children who play and learn to burn off high energy in constructive ways are more refreshed, focused, and ready to learn when asked to return to the day's more guided aspects.

There are many other forms of rest for a child. Kindergarten used to have mandatory nap time. I'm not sure how many schools still do that. The primary goal of the rest period is to take a break from all of that thinking. It is essential that development environments create sufficient time frames for resting the mind in between all the bright, beautiful bursts of learning and creativity. It is also essential for the success of the Wylde Loop.

> **CHILDREN WHO PLAY AND LEARN TO BURN OFF HIGH ENERGY IN CONSTRUCTIVE WAYS ARE MORE REFRESHED, FOCUSED, AND READY TO LEARN.**

As we talked about in chapter 5, when our imagination and creativity become blocked, we often begin to double down and push ourselves into frustration and exhaustion. We begin to work against ourselves, and the brain rebels rather than assists. We want to train this mindset into permanent brain patterns that we will carry for the rest of our lives. It's not just a break; it's a tool. When we are stuck, walk away for a moment, get a breath of fresh air, give the mind a rest, look for different options, and then come back refreshed. Yeah, yeah, sounds simple, doesn't it? How many people do you think actually use this technique beyond just vegging out, staring at their phones, or going to sleep and repeating the same process the next day?

REFRESH

How do we fill the mind with lots of good information, build powerful new connections, develop alternative ways of thinking, and improve our chances of true Creative Intelligence?

This is where parents and teachers *earn* that incredible value we talked about earlier. There is so much incredible potential in the four hours per day that we hope to develop Creative Intelligence, but it requires a highly competent, well-trained, and motivated leader. In this section, we will go through the myriad of ways in which we inspire activities, thought patterns, habits, and ignite the imagination.

> **Notes before we start:** Remember that experiential learning has at its core *experience*. Experiences matter. The more fun the better; the more exciting the better. We are trying to create a set of varied experiences that build wide, deep connections throughout the brain's architecture, implant incredible amounts of knowledge throughout our memory, and gain access and control over all parts of the brain. Exercises create connections and memories. Repetition creates patterns. Patterns become habits. With all this repetition, it is easy for us to fall back into the trap of routines and going through the motions. Our challenge is to keep these experiences fresh and entertaining in some form. While the Wylde Loops and Wylde Method are a framework for Creative Intelligence, the parent or the teacher is the mechanism by which these loops succeed. Mix it up. Invent. Try new things. There are no rules, only guidelines. All activities should be age-appropriate and increasingly challenging. Lessons, games, and exercises for five and six-year-olds will not be the same for nine and ten-year-olds. We need to help children explore and expand.

Structured play

You thought I was done with play. Not even close. Children have lots of options.

Games

Teacher-led periods of the development environment should include a variety of games. As I have repeated, we do this so well when they are little: Duck-Duck Goose, Red Light-Green

Light, musical chairs. With so much of the "academic" day now removed, we have so much more time for games. As children age through the early development, we should be creating and playing new games that challenge them to cultivate their skills, such as

- games that require physical challenges. A favorite example of mine for little ones is trying to keep up with "Head, shoulders, knees, and toes."
- games that require mental agility and rapid thinking, like "Simon Says".
- games of memory. A giant memory board is played as a team challenge where children take two sheets of paper and draw two of each item, one per sheet of paper. Spread out the papers across the ground. Children play in teams to try to accumulate the most pairs.
- silly games like Twister, Charades, or one of my favorites, "Bug in Your Pants," which you can find on our YouTube Channel.
- sensory games. For example, blindfold the child, who tries to guess what object they are holding or a noise they are listening to.
- games that require imagination, like "What happens next?" or "Let's all pretend we're flying a plane." Take turns selecting the pilot, co-pilot, passengers, and flight attendants. Imagine take-off, landing, food service, and even "crashing" for fun.

Games have unlimited options. If we put our minds to it, we have hundreds of ways to make children think, adapt, move, and laugh through games.

This is a great place to mention a book I came across in my research, titled *Range* by David Epstein. In the book, Epstein argues that generalists who explore various interests and skills are better at finding fulfilling paths and develop greater creativity and problem-solving abilities, especially in dynamic environments. My favorite part of the book is when Epstein discusses what he calls *kind* and *wicked* environments. He describes kind environments as ones with clear rules and feedback loops, meaning success is easier to follow if you know the rules, acquire the skills, and play the game well. He describes wicked environments as having few rules and a weak feedback loop, making success far more difficult. I agree with Epstein's ideas that the world we are entering will have "wicked" characteristics in that the rules will bend furiously, and all children will be forced to reckon with constant change.

I mention this within the section on games because, in addition to exploration, we are also developing skills to fit the next century. Part of Creative Intelligence will be the ability to adapt quickly to the emerging changes and set new courses of action. As leaders in the development environment, it is important that we find games and activities where we change the rules on the fly so that children can experience change within a practice environment and learn to adjust. Repeatedly placing them in these positions at an early age will teach them to stay calm, manage fear and frustration, and think of a way around the change. Children who have adopted these skill sets will be far more resilient and successful in the new era.

Sports

I am a big fan of sports and what they offer: physical skill sets, mental toughness, teamwork, collaboration, resilience, and many other benefits. Both individual and team sports can be vital to a child's personal development. As we completely change the standard educational system, one of the challenges will be to preserve the great traditions of after-school sports. We should make every effort to maintain these opportunities for those who *gravitate* toward a love of sport.

I would caution the discussion with the idea of balance in mind. In the early years, we need to make sure that the pursuit of sports does not come at the cost of developing other skills and traits of Creative Intelligence. Every year, parents spend thousands of hours and tons of money trying to develop the next Tiger Woods, Lebron James, or Roger Federer. I am especially concerned with the notion that, for many in less fortunate communities, professional sports is seen as "the only way out." I understand that some children are prodigious or exceptionally talented. However, I would refrain from overscheduling and obsessive pursuit in these important years of development.

Despite your best efforts, not many children are meant to be superstar athletes. Ask yourself a few questions. Is the time and investment healthy for your child? Is it self-driven and intrinsically motivated? Did they choose to pursue the sport, or did you? Last, but not least, at what cost? Are we depriving them of other opportunities for exploration and development? Is there even time for anything else? Is your child excited, engaged, and ignited when playing or practicing? Or are they tired, grumpy, and complaining about practice?

Exploration

The broader the experience, the better. The world is a vast place. Part of our goal is to enhance the big database we draw upon for the process of imagination and creativity. The more sources of potential information, the more options there are for new ideas and connections. The better part of exploration is the beauty of life itself. Beyond facts, the opportunity exists to inform knowledge with texture, add colors and contrasts, variations and options, broaden our perspectives and horizons, and understand people and cultures. There is no end to what we can see, learn, and experience. Again, losing the extreme focus on test-prep-test gives us so much more time to explore.

Bring back the arts!

There, I said it. They should never have been cancelled in the first place. The influence of art on a child's development is priceless. I don't understand how we ever got to the point where the idea took hold that pursuing the arts was a waste of time. Studying the arts *improves* academic performance. More importantly, they offer a broader and more holistic development of the brain's creative capacities and social connections. The arts enhance cognitive skills, problem-solving, and memory. They can improve motor skills and hand-eye coordination. Working on art projects can improve focus, perseverance, discipline, and resilience. Perhaps greatest of all, the arts can provide the opportunity for personal expression and self-confidence born out of the act of creation. This can be especially powerful for children who are not physically inclined or academically gifted.

- Music: In addition to fun and silly songs, children should be exposed to classical, folk, rock, and other modern forms of music. They should be introduced to all types of instruments and be given the opportunity to play them. Music can be used in the background to quiet the room or pump up motivation during game

- Dance: I am an aficionado of all kinds of dance. I wish that every young girl or boy who wanted could try jazz, hip hop, and ballet in formal settings. But even in informal settings, dance has incredible power. Children should be exposed to everything from a "dance party" free-for-all to line dancing. Imagine the fun of trying to keep a group of five-year-olds in step to a tune. You can ask kids to make up their own dances.
- Visual Arts: What does a child see when he or she looks at art by Picasso? What about Monet or Dali? Children can be introduced to the masters or just paint with their fingers. They can be taught visual graphics or learn how Disney animators create their favorite characters. They can paint, draw, construct, and build art in a variety of ways.
- Drama: Most people think of drama as a high-school activity. While the full scope of theater may be left for children older than our target group, there are plenty of ways to use the power of drama to inspire and enhance the development environment. On a broader scope, so many of the biggest productions have been redeveloped for children. I believe every child should have the opportunity to see celebrated Broadway shows like *The Lion King*, *Mary Poppins*, *Aladdin*, and *Matilda*, even if it is only through streaming or the internet. In addition, tons of children's theater pieces

> **THE EXERCISE OF PRETENDING OPENLY IN FRONT OF GROUPS OF PEOPLE IN FUN WAYS CAN DEVELOP TREMENDOUS CONFIDENCE AND SOCIAL SKILLS.**

can be extrapolated for fun: *A Christmas Carol*, *The Wizard of Oz*, and *Peter Pan*. The heart of drama is the art of pretending, a skill that nearly every single child holds naturally and with abundance. The exercise of pretending openly in front of groups of people in fun ways can develop tremendous confidence and social skills. In addition, traditional drama instruction has a variety of drills and techniques, such as vocalization and improvisation, to help build agility, adaptability, and presence.

Languages

Children should be introduced to a wide range of languages in early development. Bilingual brains often show increased grey matter density and stronger neural connections, resulting in increased cognitive flexibility. Understanding more than one language improves critical thinking, memory, and attention. Learning languages acts as a mental workout, enhancing the brain's ability to switch between tasks or topics. Hearing different languages enhances sensory reception and interpretation. Speaking different languages affects recall and connection. My suggestion isn't necessarily that we take up tons of development time mastering multiple languages. Parents may choose to do so at home, and children may opt to continue learning based on their own desire. My main suggestion during the early development phase is to *expose* children to different sounds and different ways of communication to broaden their cultural experiences and perspectives. It can be as simple as doing the ABCs in four languages or identifying an apple in five.

All the senses

There are five senses: sight, sound, touch, smell, and taste. Children should have as many sensory experiences as humanly possible during development. What does an alpaca fur feel like? What about a horseshoe crab? How many colors does a butterfly come in? Have you ever felt one in your hand? What's a scorpion look like up close? What does the ocean smell like? What about cow dung? What does lemon meringue pie taste like? How does it feel in the mouth? What about a cocoa bean? Why does sugar make everything taste better? How do they make perfumes? Does a crocodile roar? How cold is it at the North Pole? How many shades of pink are there? What do bare feet feel like on wood, stone, crushed marble, carpet, snow, grass, hot sand, and soft wool? Can you tell the difference between the sound of rain and a water faucet? Every sight, sound, touch, taste, and smell a child experiences expands their database and connections. The more experiences, the more robust the choices. Explore, explore, explore.

Nature

Are we giving children sufficient connection to the natural world? Children need to explore grass, trees, rivers, lakes, oceans, and forests. They need to experience animals and creatures in the wild, on farms, and in zoos. They need to feel the wind and the rain and the sun. They need to learn in the outside world whenever possible. If there are no big opportunities for exploring nature, we should give them smaller ones, like walking in a field and looking for bugs, or gardening and growing vegetables. If there are no forests, oceans, or mountains nearby, we should do whatever we can to bring them inside. Bring animals into the classroom. Bring plants, acorns, pinecones, and seashells into the classroom.

History, geography, and culture

I hate to say it, but this is one of the major failures of the modern educational system. Kids are graduating from high school without being able to identify entire continents or nations on a map. They can tell you who got kicked off "Love Island," but they can't tell you who fought at the Battle of the Little Bighorn, or who invented penicillin. Again, we don't want to bind children with a bunch of history lessons followed by intense testing. The entire idea is exploration in fun and exciting ways. When facts are interesting or introduced in a fascinating manner, they will make their way into the accessible parts of memory. Being exposed to people, places, foods, traditions, architecture, and stories from around the world endlessly expands the database in our minds and offers up millions of connections available for discovery.

Who created French fries? Did Italy create pizza? Where was flamenco dancing born? What language do they speak in Cambodia? Where is Chinese food from? Where did the Wright brothers fly their airplane? What did a map of Europe look like in 1700? Where are most castles located? Why do Russians wear furry hats? How was chocolate invented? Who was Poseidon? Is there really a Bigfoot? What's the difference between Argentina and Chile? Or Peru, for that matter. Where are the Caribbean islands? Where are the Hawaiian Islands? Where are the Greek Islands? Where are the Canary Islands? Where can I swim with the dolphins?

Science

First, science is way cool. There are few better ways to ignite a child's curiosity, imagination, and excitement than by doing fun, teachable science experiments. Teachers can go online or watch YouTube channels, like Mark Rober and others, and come away with hundreds of super fun experiments for all ages.

Second, every child who wants to develop Creative Intelligence should learn the basis for the scientific method at an early age: observe, ask questions, gather information, form a hypothesis, test the hypothesis, assess the data and results, come to a conclusion, and communicate the outcome. This process has always been groundbreaking in its ability to power innovation and can be used in a variety of ways.

Project-based learning

One of the greatest ways to put all of the exploration together and build additional skill sets is to engage in project-based learning, both on an individual level and in collaborative teams. In the development environment, it is the primary way in which we move from the imaginative to the creative stage. Projects help develop the core and function of Creative Intelligence. This is the spine or vehicle in which we practice the full challenges of the Wylde Loop. These can be teacher-led in the earliest years, but should be increasingly autonomous as the children learn to effectively manage their own time and efforts. By initiating projects, we give children multiple opportunities to practice and absorb the following key skills and traits:

- Developing a North Star. What is the vision for this project? What are we trying to create or solve? *Creative Thinking/Problem-Solving/Agency*
- Devising a plan. How do we think we can accomplish this? *Strategic Thinking/Communication*
- Breaking down larger goals into smaller, achievable activities. *Creative Thinking/Problem-Solving*
- Needs Assessment. What items do we need to complete this project? How will we acquire them? *Strategic Thinking/Problem-Solving*
- Lateral thinking. How many different ways can we think of to solve the same problem? What happens when we get stuck? *Creative Thinking/Alternative Thinking/Problem-Solving/Collaboration/Imagination*
- Teamwork and division of labor. What does each team member do well? How should we divide up the work? What happens when partners disagree? *Collaboration/Communication/Social Skills/Conflict Resolution*
- Rapid learning curves. Is there anything we will need to learn to complete this project? *Curiosity/Adaptability/Problem Solving/Agency/Agility*
- Risk-taking. Implement the plan. *Bias Toward Action/Confidence*
- Assessment and Iteration. What happens when we fail? What went wrong? What adjustments do we make? What would we do differently this time around? Let's try it again. *Critical Thinking/Problem-Solving/Creative Thinking/Lateral thinking/Focus/Discipline/Perseverance/Resilience/Adaptability/Imagination*
- Project Completion. *Confidence/Mastery/Responsibility/Self-Efficacy/Agency/Pride/Enhanced Knowledge/Love of Learning/Social and Human Connection.*

Imagine how much empowerment we create by replacing hours of sitting in chairs looking forward or staring down with collaborative teams solving real problems and achieving outcomes on a consistent basis.

> **Build and Play:** Before we leave this section, I want to mention one of the greatest single toys ever created for children that provides a foundation for imagination and creativity—the LEGO brick. In its simplest form, the LEGO brick is a micro environment for building something. It brings to mind Mitchel Resnick's message: "Creators must create." The LEGO brick can be used in many different ways across the Wylde Loop:
>
> - REST—As a simple form of relaxed play.
> - REFRESH—The art of planning, building, practicing, analyzing, tearing down, and rebuilding.
> - REIMAGINE—There is no better "blank page" exercise than handing a child a bucket of LEGO bricks and leaving them alone without any instructions or goals.
>
> They can be used alone, with friends, or in project-based activities.
>
> Equally impressive to me has been the company's efforts to build out an incredibly simple foundation into a tool set that provides play and learning for many different age groups with ever-increasing age-appropriate challenges in a variety of ways. There are simple versions for the very youngest of explorers. There are increasingly more complicated sets that incorporate STEAM, including science, construction, engineering, and robotics. They use and

> create characters and worlds that engross children and give the bricks meaning and color. They have dedicated entire divisions and product lines to promoting education and supporting teachers.
>
> There are many available toys and kits designed to ignite imagination and exploration for these age groups. I recommend that all learning environments be equipped with hands-on, interactive, build-and-create tools. Few, however, are as simple and have as much potential as a good old-fashioned set of LEGO bricks.

REIMAGINE

Ok, so we've walked through what stepping away from thinking looks like and how to fill our minds with wonderful new information, connections, and ideas. We've also practiced the art of applying our wonderful intelligence through consistent project-based activities, games, and challenges. But what about the deepest forms of creativity? What do we do when the breakthrough we are looking for just won't appear?

The answer is simple: *it's time to do nothing*.

Everything we have discussed above is either taking a break from the active pursuit of a problem or using our conscious mind and efforts to solve the problem. Remember, however, that the deepest levels of imagination need help from our subconscious. Sometimes sleep helps. But let's discuss some other ways we can move toward daydreaming within the development environment.

Walks: In 335 BC, Aristotle, one of the great Greek philosophers, created the Peripatetic school, which referred to the practice of teachers and students conversing while walking. Two thousand years later, and there are fewer great ways to get your mind to start wandering. This is often done best alone or in silence. Walking distracts your mind by forcing it into minimal energy and focus, keeping you grounded just enough to allow for the remaining energy to wander freely. Imagine a line of first graders, lined up like ducks behind a teacher, walking in the school yard, hands clasped behind their backs, pondering.

The Blank Page: Hand children a blank piece of paper and a pen or crayons, and give absolutely no instructions. Just let them sit for thirty minutes and draw or write what comes to mind.

Quiet Time: One of the greatest challenges for all human beings is the ability to handle silence. We are supercharged at all times and addicted to stimulation. The same restlessness that drives abuse of cell phones is the one that blocks your subconscious from rising. For children to tap into the subconscious at will and become highly creative, they must become comfortable with the silence in their minds. The only way to become powerful at this is to train it into their hardwiring at a very young age. All development environments should create purposeful periods of zero activity at increasing time periods. Start small when they are small. By the time they are ten, all children should be able to operate in silence for at least thirty minutes without disruption.

Simple Prompts: Your subconscious brain has the ability to work in the background, even if we are engaged in more conscious efforts. It's why so many moments of inspiration occur at the most unexpected times. One of my favorite ways is to keep the brain considering ideas and searching for connections at all times. I call this prompting. Children should constantly be given prompts that lead them to imagine. We are not expecting answers right away or ever. It's a simple mind trick to keep their mind working for connections. For example, after a fun day talking about pirates, send them home with the following. "When you go home tonight, I want you to imagine your life as a pirate." Or before a period of silence, give them a prompt like, "See if you can think of a fun game for all of us to do tomorrow." The trick is to do this often, and if possible, right before they have time to relax the mind.

REENGAGEMENT

If we have done our job well in the first three phases of the Wylde Loop, this last step is the easiest part. Our minds are relaxed. We are full of exciting new information and ideas. We have imagined new solutions and approaches. We are guided by North Stars. We are resilient. We are motivated and driven back to the active pursuit of our mission under our own accord. We have passion and purpose behind our sails. We are capable of creating anything, especially value.

The ultimate goal of the development environment is the cross-fertilization and pollination of all the different forms of experience listed above. The full cycle experience of the Wylde Loop may look something like this.

- The focus of the day is life on Mars.
- We watch a rocket launch on TV and learn about SpaceX.
- The teacher leads an open discussion on what everyone thinks life on Mars would be like. What would be fun?

What would be hard? What would the challenges be? How would we eat?
- Everyone separates into teams and begins a competition to build a rocket ship out of a limited set of materials. Older kids lead younger ones in simpler arts and craft models.
- The entire school goes outside to watch the launch of a model rocket, built and launched by the older kids.
- Older kids are challenged to reach out to SpaceX and build connections.
- We send kids home with a prompt, not homework: "Would you want to be one of the first people to live on Mars?"

From play to passion to purpose. I also believe in the concept of "go big or go home." How exciting can we make this experience? How big can the lesson get? I mentioned a rocket launch in the schoolyard above. What about a school-wide domino toppling competition, where everyone in the school is challenged with creating an exciting domino pattern, and the winners recreate their pattern in the gym for everyone to watch topple? Rather than sitting in chairs for seven to eight hours, dying to check our social media accounts or go home and play video games, we are playing, imagining, exploring, testing, assessing, and iterating day in and day out, over and over again, until all of the skill sets needed to thrive in the age of robots and artificial intelligence are baked in and second nature. We can call upon them in any situation and adapt to any change. Most of all, we carry with us powerful imaginations.

Here's a simpler way of looking at it.

- Every day, a child should be shown love, kindness, and compassion.

- Every day, a child should read.
- Every day, a child should have unstructured play for two to three hours.
- Every day, a child should be prompted to imagine.
- Every day, a child should be given time to daydream.
- Every day, a child should be encouraged to explore.
- Every day, a child should be given the opportunity to create.
- Every day, a child should learn something new.
- Every day, a child should experience fun and laughter.
- Every day, a child should be challenged to new heights.
- Every day, a child should connect and build human connections with others.
- I know it sounds like a wish list; it's not. It's a set of priorities.

A FEW WORDS FROM THE AUTHOR

HUMANITY'S LAST STAND.

When I speak of preserving humanity...

In this new century, we will have to find a way to see every possible route through, around, and over every challenge and obstacle our own ingenuity creates. We will be forced to innovate and counter-innovate to survive, but also to thrive.

We need children with vivid imaginations who are endlessly curious and tirelessly creative. We need to develop children who have autotelic and autodidactic personalities. We need children who can think independently and determine their own purpose in life. We need children who can finish what they start, regardless of how difficult the path is. And not least of all, we will need to create active participants in society who are kind, compassionate, and wholly committed to human connection.

Quite frankly, this is the opposite of the generational challenges we have seen unfold over the last twenty to thirty years. Children lack resilience and initiative. Somehow, with the most knowledge available in history, they are poorly informed and easily misled. Many are isolated in echo chambers and lack social skills. Through the anonymity of social media, they have developed a lack of compassion and empathy for fellow human beings, instead exhibiting a narcissistic form of virtue signaling that prioritizes indirect action and passive engagement over direct action and active engagement.

Humans will not survive if we go down this path. Living life through a narrow window of convenience and abundance without responsibility and self-determination will only result in weaker and more isolated individuals. Why and how would anyone develop into positive, active human beings in a world where you never have to leave the house, when all your needs are fulfilled, and actions lack consequences? If you desire, you'd never have to think again beyond your own current base desires.

I believe in the power of possibilities and the wonderful world of abundance that awaits the other side of this transformation. However, the speed of change and the power of technology have the potential to pull the rug out from under all of us collectively, leaving us lying on our backs and wondering what just happened. All our most brilliant minds openly admit that we are in the middle of a new Manhattan Project. Like the power, promises, and dangers of a nuclear age, we must gather to build a framework that will safeguard generations to come. Of all the possible solutions to the challenges of the future, none is more powerful than this: the bold imagination of a single child.

WYLDE SCOTT

What's with the Blue Hat?

Wylde Scott was born on a mountaintop
Somewhere between the beginning of time
And the clock's bell last night
His father was the stars and his mother the wind
They say he was born with a mischievous grin

WYLDE SCOTT

He was raised by a band of gypsies
Who taught him to sing and play and dance
and walk and skip on the palms of his hands

He has lived and traveled all over the world
From Shanghai to Kalamazoo
To Bangkok and Timbuktu
And still has a house on the bright side of the moon

He is a Sultan and a Matador
And Knight through and through
But mostly he loves telling stories
To wide-eyed, big dreaming, belly-giggling children
Just like you

If you haven't realized this yet, Wylde Scott is a pseudonym. My favorite description of what I imagined with Wylde Scott is well described in Todd Harman's book *The Alter Ego Effect*. What Harman describes is really a form of modeling. He utilizes the idea of children putting on a Superman cape to better prepare and perform in the world. The cape itself is defined as the perfect example of the person you are trying to be, and the act of putting it on is the act of transformation. I have been doing this for many years.

When I place the Blue Hat on my head, it serves as a reminder that I am stepping into the world of children. It is a total transformation of the person into the ideal children's character. I wanted to create a character who is kind, compassionate, and safe for children. The character needed to be wildly funny and fun to be with. He needed to be highly imaginative, capable of pulling thousands of surprises from his hat. He needed to hold deep words of wisdom without ever letting the spark of childhood go. I wanted him to be a beautiful storyteller in the likes of Hans Christian Andersen, the Brothers Grimm, Roald Dahl, and Dr. Seuss. He had to be a strong protector of children. Above all, I wanted him to represent the imagination. When a child of any age comes into contact with Wylde, they are experiencing imagination itself.

As a children's brand, our mission is to deliver fun, entertaining, age-appropriate, and safe educational content based on imagination and play. In addition to our current books, we will be publishing a long line of picture books, chapter books, and novels for early readers, followed by streaming content, television, and film.

If you have young children, please consider subscribing to our YouTube channel, @wyldescottvideos, buying our books, and following us on social media.

We look forward to having you join us on the journey of Imagination.

THE IMAGINATION PROJECT

Years ago, as I launched our first book and began to visit schools across the country, I was invited to a small elementary school in the far reaches of Brooklyn, NY. A teacher had raised just enough funds for me to travel there and cover the hotel room. I donated books to help the school raise funds, and she hustled in other ways to bring it all together. The students were mostly immigrants from lesser-known parts of Central and Latin America, along with others normally found in inner-city, poorly-resourced schools. Two live sessions had been set up, one for K–2 and another for grades 3–5. We were still in the early stages of developing our events, and I was excited to be there. As we waited in between the first and second sessions, eating a piece of pizza, the teacher turned to me and said, "Thank you for coming here." I was humbled for even being invited, much less knowing the hard work she had done on behalf of her students. She was one of the "great" teachers I love to talk about, who really cared. "Thank you for inviting me," I responded. She looked at me again and said, "No, really. Thank you for coming. *No one ever comes here.*"

Those words broke my heart. I have never been able to forget them. Without dragging this book into my own childhood, *I was that child.* I came from a broken home with few resources and was raised in the middle of a poor community. I knew exactly what it was like to struggle and feel like no one cared. Deep down, I always knew it was a significant part of why I needed to become Wylde Scott. My own journey began to transform as I visited more and more schools. The vast difference between affluent programs in beautiful neighborhoods with vibrant PTAs and the less fortunate schools with little community support or resources became all too visible. What began as a journey of promotion became a mission of passion. We began to visit any school that needed us, giving away thousands of books for free when children could not afford them.

We created The Imagination Project to expand our ability to serve children, schools, and communities that no one ever visits. Our mission is to ignite a fire of imagination in their young minds that cannot be extinguished. We do live events designed to inspire and empower dreaming. We give away books to improve literacy and ensure they take these messages home at night. We dream of sending deserving kids to camps and adventures they themselves would otherwise never experience.

With the age of artificial intelligence upon us and the publication of this book, we hope to advance the cause even further. You see, children with an abundance of resources and support will adapt. We already see the right types of innovation in places like the Alpha School. Children born into the families of technology leadership will be on the cutting edge of what works and what doesn't. They will pick and choose what schools their kids go to and what technologies they will be allowed to use. But what about everyone else? We know in great transformations like this, it's the less fortunate who are left behind. My greatest concern is the further separation of society, with entire communities permanently lost in translation. Those same systems are generally the most underfunded, highly bureaucratic, and the hardest to turn. For all the reasons I have discussed in this book, we can't let that happen. It's our responsibility to take action rather than look away.

At The Imagination Project, we don't just want to inspire and empower less fortunate children; we want to give them the tools to succeed in their own future. As part of our goals, we want to help school districts and communities across the world adapt educational models and systems to the speed and needs of the twenty-first century. We want to empower and instruct teachers on how to build enormous, powerful imaginations and Creative Intelligence. We want to help transform testing laboratories designed in the industrial era into vibrant development environments. With your help, we can ensure an entire generation of children is prepared to meet their future.

If you'd like to help, go to ImaginationProject.org to learn more.

REFERENCES AND RESOURCES

BOOKS

Rubin, Rick. *The Creative Act: A way of Being.* New York: Penguin, 2023.

Robinson, Sir Ken. *Out of Our Minds: The Power of Being Creative.* New York: John Wiley & Sons, 2011.

Robinson, Sir Ken. *Creative Schools: The Grassroots Revolution That's Transforming Education.* New York: Penguin, 2015.

Csikszentmihalyi, Mihaly. *Flow: The Psychology of Optimal Experience.* New York: Harper Perennial, 1990.

Csikszentmihalyi, Mihaly. *The Psychology of Discovery and Invention.* New York: Harper Perennial, 1996.

Catmull, Ed. *Creativity, Inc: Overcoming Unseen Forces that Stand in the Way of True Inspiration.* New York: Bantam, 2014.

Wagner, Tony. *Creating Innovators: The Making of Young People Who Will Change the World.* New York: Scribner, 2012.

Siegel, Daniel J. *The Developing Mind: How Relationships and the Brain Interact to Shape Who We Are.* New York: Guilford, 2020.

Siegel, Daniel J. *The Developing Mind: How Relationships and the Brain Interact to Shape Who We Are.* New York: Guilford, 2020.

Siegel, Daniel J. and Tina Payne Bryson. *The Whole-Brain Child: 12 Revolutionary Strategies to Nurture Your Child's Developing Mind.* New York: New York: Bantam, 2011.

Elkind, David. *The Power of Play: Learning What Comes Naturally.* Boston: Da Capo Lifelong, 2007.

Epstein, David. *Range: Why Generalists Triumph in a Specialized World.* New York: Riverhead Books, 2019.

Hermann, Todd. *The Alter Ego Effect: Defeat the Enemy, Unlock Your Heroic Self, and Start Kicking Ass.* New York: Harper, 2019.

Brown, Stuart. *Play: How It Shapes the Brain, Opens the Imagination and Invigorates the Soul.* New York: Avery, 2010.

Apter, Terry. *The Confident Child: Raising Children to Believe in Themselves.* New York: Norton, 1997.

Andreasen, Nancy C. *The Creative Brain: The Science of Genius.* New York: Plume, 2005.

Haidt, Jonathan. *The Anxious Generation: How the Great Rewiring of Childhood Is Causing an Epidemic of Mental Illness.* New York: Penguin, 2024.

ENDNOTES

1. Tristan Harris. "Why AI Is Our Ultimate Test and Greatest Invitation." TedTalk, April 9, 2025. https://youtu.be/6kPHnl-RsVI?si=ZDOXo9AvSl1t76WS.
2. Csikszentmihalyi, Mihaly. Flow. New York: Harper, 2008, 3.
3. Csikszentmihalyi, 225.
4. Ken Robinson. Creative Schools: The Grassroots Revolution That's Transforming Education. New York: Penguin, 2015.
5. Siegel, Daniel J. and Tina Payne Bryson The Whole-Brain Child: 12 Revolutionary Strategies to Nurture Your Child's Developing Mind. New York: Bantam, 2012, 100-102.
6. Csikszentmihalyi, Flow, 26.
7. Siegel, 77.
8. Andrey Vyshedskiy, "The Science of Imagination," TED-Ed, 2016, https://www.youtube.com/watch?v=e7uXAlXdTe4.
9. Mihaly Csikszentmihalyi, Creativity: The Psychology of Discovery and Invention (New York: Harper, 2013, 101.
10. Siegel, 122.
11. Ruder, Ella. "The US behavioral health market, 2025 to 2038: 8 things to know." Becker's Behavioral Health. September 10,

2025. https://www.beckersbehavioralhealth.com/behavioral-health-capital-investment/the-u-s-behavioral-health-market-2025-to-2034-8-things-to-know/.

12 Rick Rubin, The Creative Act: A Way of Being (New York: Penguin, 2023), 8-9.

13 Robinson, Ken Robinson. "Do Schools Kill Creativity?" Ted. Youtube. 2007. https://youtu.be/iG9CE55wbtY?si=tFl9wU3Q2veazqYI.

14 Robinson, Ken. Out of Our Minds: The Power of Being Creative. North Mankato, MN: Capstone, 2017, 46.

15 Robinson, Creative Schools, xvi.

16 Robinson, Creative Schools, xxii.

17 Robinson, Creative Schools, 8.

18 Brian Stieglitz, "College costs increase 169% since 1980 to between $27,000 and $55,000 per year but salaries for graduates increase by only 19%," DailyMail.com, https://www.dailymail.co.uk/news/article-10162761/College-costs-increase-169-1980-salaries-graduates-increase-19.html.

19 Marcus, Jon. "Grad programs have been a cash cow; now universities are starting to fret over graduate enrollment." The Hechinger Report. June 10, 2024. https://hechingerreport.org/as-undergraduate-numbers-slide-universities-start-to-fret-over-graduate-enrollment/.

20 Hanson, Melanie., "Student Loan Dept Statistics." Education Data Initiative. Accessed December 5, 2025. https://educationdata.org/student-loan-debt-statistics.

21 Robinson, Creative Schools, xxii.

22 Haidt, Jonathan Haidt The Anxious Generation. New York: Penguin, 2024.

23 Burn-Murdoch, John. "The troubling decline in conscienciousness." Financial Times. August 8, 2025. https://www.ft.com/content/5cd77ef0-b546-4105-8946-36db3f84dc43.
24 Robinson, Creative Schools, 154.

ACKNOWLEDGMENTS

I would like to thank my business partners Michael Jefferson and Ryan "Flash" Bennett, without whom this book would not have been possible.

I would also like to thank Tony Colson and my team at Igniting Souls for their help in preparing this book for publication.

And a thank you to Spencer Podolski for helping me share this book with the world.

One final note…

I am a children's author. I have been focused on imagination for more than thirty years. First, my own, then the imaginations of children. The foundation of this book was built from years of research, play, writing, and interaction with thousands of young children in schools, libraries, bookstores, and personal environments. I have read nearly every book about creative writing, theater, television, characters, and imagination. I am, however, not a neurologist, biologist, psychologist, sociologist, anthropologist, or any other formally known type of ologist. Neither do I have a master's nor a PhD in education. I am simply an observer of human beings, particularly children. At best, I might be considered a highly trained Imaginologist.

To take on this book and expand its range into the worlds of education, childhood development, the brain, and artificial intelligence, I have relied on the experience and expertise of many others. I have added many more books, articles, white papers, and research papers to my mental framework. Throughout the chapters, I have tried to document every idea and concept that has greatly influenced my opinions and provided guidance for this book by referencing the authors, books, and sources directly. Included in these pages are a thousand hours of new media, including podcasts, interviews, conferences, Google searches, and discussions with teachers and parents, all with the goal of informing my work.

What I hope will happen as a result of this book is that professionals from all fields will join me in prioritizing Imagination and Creative Intelligence, add to the conversation, and help revolutionize education throughout the world. The time is now. The need is urgent. We will need an army of parents, teachers, educators, psychologists, neurologists, technologists, scientists, and more as we move through the greatest transformation in the history of the world. Let's work together to preserve humanity.

Thank you for your support and for taking the time to read this book.

SUBSCRIBE TO OUR YOUTUBE CHANNEL FOR KIDS!

Join Wylde as he brings magical energy to children from ages 2-8 in the form of safe, educational and exciting videos based in imagination and play.

YouTube.com/@WyldeScottVideos

Interested In Learning More About Creating A Wild and Exciting Learning Environment?

Subscribe to our Wylde Parents and Teachers YouTube Channel

Here, we will expand on raising Dreamers with guides, games, tips and tricks for creating exciting experiential learning environments.

YouTube.com/@WyldeParentsandTeachers

Invite Wylde Scott To Speak Today!

Light up your conference or event with fun insights on the imagination and building Wylde, creative environments for children of all ages.

We offer exciting events for children as well as engaging and interactive training for teachers.

WyldeScott.com/contact

CONNECT WITH WYLDE SCOTT

Follow him on your favorite social media platforms today.

WyldeScott.com

Enjoy Wylde's Other Books

Ages 3-6

Ages 7-12

AVAILABLE WHEREVER BOOKS ARE SOLD